"Louis Hernandez, Jr., is one of the true visionaries in the media industry today, and his new book is reflecting his vision and passion to cultivate a better environment for content creators to excel. He turns the media industry inside out, as he delves into the impact technology has had—good and bad—on a flailing media industry, and by doing so, has given us all a new way of looking at storytelling, then and now, and what we must do to revitalize the industry and keep the true art form of storytelling alive!"

—Daniel Fung, chairman and CEO, NDT (Hong Kong, China)

"The Storyteller's Dilemma is a penetrating analysis of where we are now in the media industry. It takes a unique viewpoint with the artistic and aesthetic at its core, and is full of original insights as well as providing a roadmap to navigate this technology-enabled acceleration of the industry."

—Fred Mattocks, general manager, CBC Canada (Toronto, Canada)

"With a clear look into reality and future outlook, Hernandez provides us with the hows and whys of the collision of new technology and outdated business models."

—Turki Aldakhil, general manager,
Alarabiya & Alhadath news channels (Dubai, United Arab Emirates)

"This book is at once challenging and fascinating. The detailed arguments reveal a depth of understanding of the intricate relationships between creativity and business in the modern world. Mr. Hernandez presents both an analysis and a rallying cry for all involved in the business of media. Not to be missed."

—Jonathan Wales, CEO,
Wildfire Sonic Magic (Los Angeles, California)

"A concise, informative, and all-around good read, *The Storyteller's Dilemma* helps everyone from the musician to the film executive to the podcast listener better navigate the seismic forces democratizing media content creation, distribution, and consumption in our digital age. It's timely and won't disappoint."

—Paula Boggs, professional musician
and former Fortune 500 executive (Seattle, Washington)

THE STORYTELLER'S
DILEMMA

THE STORYTELLER'S
DILEMMA

OVERCOMING THE CHALLENGES IN THE DIGITAL MEDIA AGE

LOUIS HERNANDEZ, JR.

HAL LEONARD BOOKS
AN IMPRINT OF HAL LEONARD LLC

Published in 2017 by Hal Leonard Books
An Imprint of Hal Leonard LLC
7777 West Bluemound Road
Milwaukee, WI 53213

Trade Book Division Editorial Offices
33 Plymouth St., Montclair, NJ 07042

Printed in the United States of America

Book design by Lynn Bergesen, UB Communications

Library of Congress Cataloging-in-Publication Data is available upon request.

ISBN: 978-1-4950-6481-4

www.halleonardbooks.com

I dedicate this book to my wife, children, and family,
who have provided the kind of unwavering support
that allows you to reach for more.

To the media professionals throughout the world,
who have dedicated their lives to sharing experiences
through storytelling.
You are a key part of the global social fabric
that connects us all and shapes our human existence.
Spending time with you and being a part
of your community is a true inspiration
that excites the soul and stimulates the senses.
I salute you!

Contents

Preface

Storytelling is fundamental to being human. We've been communicating emotions and ideas for almost as long as we've been on the planet, through visual art, music, and language. The urge to create and share is intrinsic to the human spirit itself—a constant companion that appears everywhere, in every age. There is undeniable joy in the connection between storyteller and audience.

Today that joy has become increasingly linked to the digital experience. The way creative people express themselves, and the way their audiences enjoy the story, has been forever changed by technology and the pervasive connectivity of the Internet. This book explores that phenomenon, along with some of the challenges that it has created.

This rush to digitization is not surprising; computing technology is simply the latest, and by far the most powerful, means we have of communicating our ideas and emotions. The creative drive is always present, but the way it plays out is inextricably linked to technology and social and economic forces. We use the resources available to us—whether they're ochre, charcoal, and plant dyes used to create a cave painting, a Stradivarius in the hands of a baroque violinist, or the latest digital audio and video production tools. Likewise, we spread our stories any way we can—through oral or religious tradition, by signing a deal with a major record label, broadcast or streaming network, playing a live show, or posting a digital file on the Internet. Throughout history, tools and methods have shaped the stories we tell, the way we tell them, and how our audience experiences them.

Today, we're at an inflection point that is the direct result of the digital revolution. In some ways the state of storytelling has never been better. Thanks to ready access to technology and connectivity, more content is being created and consumed than at any other time in human history. It's easier than ever for artists to produce and share their work. And with the emergence of virtual and augmented reality, storytelling is taking on a whole new dimension. As consumers, we are awash in choice, prices are low, and access is just a click or swipe away.

But at the same time, we face a crisis. Technology, human behavior, and economics have come together in a kind of perfect storm that makes it all but impossible to make a living as a content creator. For example, to make $1,000 in music, a signed artist with an assumed revenue share of 23 percent would need to sell 362 CDs[1] at the average price of $12.00 per CD. If that artist's distribution is solely through single-track sales via a platform like iTunes, and revenue share is assumed to be the same, he or she would need to sell 4,392 track downloads priced at $0.99 per song[2] to make that same $1,000. In terms of streaming, depending on the service, it can take anywhere from 100,000 to 1 million streams[3] to make the same few dollars. Even though streaming service revenues have increased more than 300 percent in the past few years, U.S. recorded music revenue has declined more than 40 percent in the last decade.[4] Clearly, the situation is out of balance, and therein lies the dilemma.

The same explosion of technology that has been so life-enriching has also added enormous complexity and cost to the media business. In order to adjust to the new reality, budgets have increased, but the balance has shifted away from funding content creation toward distribution and monetization. This economics-driven shift is understandable, but it isn't good. It's unsustainable, and it's getting worse.

Does that spell doom? Of course not. As long as mothers tell bedtime stories to their babies, as long as people sing, as long as musicians play and actors act, as long as communities share local news and humans have a need to share common experiences, storytelling will endure. And the media industry that brings those stories to the world will continue to play a vital role in the fabric of society. But we should be concerned, and we should act.

Creativity—and by extension, great content—blossoms when people have the means and incentive to express themselves. The reverse is equally true. That's why we should all care deeply about the current state of affairs and where we go from here. The actions we take, as content creators, consumers, media professionals, businesspeople, and legislators, will make a real difference.

Where are we, how did we get here, and what should we do about it? That's what this book is about. It is a tale of innovation yielding unanticipated outcomes. It's about the undeniable power and romance of storytelling and an examination of the forces shaping the digital world that consumes so much of our attention. More importantly, it is a call for a new path, one that is simpler, fairer, and more open—and that can be sustained. Ultimately we must find the right balance so that this generation and those to come will be able to embrace the joy of storytelling and the power it has to shape who we are. The question is how.

This isn't simply another demand for wealth redistribution so that artists can get their fair share, nor is it a review of the dislocation caused by digital distribution, or even a critique of the "big business" that media has become. These are just a few aspects of a very complex issue. Rather, it's a vision of a new approach that benefits everyone—a way to embrace the intensifying power of storytelling so that it continues to inspire and excite us, without the unnecessary disequilibrium so often experienced by industries in transition. That's important, because if one group gains only at the expense of others, we're not solving anything—merely creating a new set of intractable problems.

Every generation must adapt to a constantly shifting landscape in which many aspects of life change dramatically as time passes. Societies and cultures evolve, and human contact changes along with them. Media is no different. It's clear that the tools of technology are allowing us to create and connect in ways that we could only imagine a decade or so ago. What role will this generation play in sustaining the power of sharing that is part of our social fabric? How will we ensure that the stories which have always provided a fundamental connection that ties us together can continue to be a vibrant, thriving part of our lives?

If we can create an environment where the business of media—whether it's television, film, music, journalism, or gaming—is streamlined and less costly, more money can go toward the creation of great content without impacting profit. That's good for business, it's good for content creators, and it's good for consumers. And that's why it matters to all of us.

THE STORYTELLER'S
DILEMMA

PART 1

In a Digital World, We All Play a Part

CHAPTER 1

The Enduring Power
of Storytelling

*We learned more from a three-minute record than we ever
learned in school.*

—Bruce Springsteen

A few years ago, I attended a charitable fund-raiser that hosted a touring exhibit of my photography. I called the exhibit *Hope, Courage, Triumph: Stories of Everyday Heroes Among Us*. The images told incredible stories by capturing the daily activities of impoverished people around the world. I believe many of us would consider these people heroic if we were to walk in their shoes for just one day.

One of the most popular photos auctioned off that evening was an image of a little boy nestled in a small, glassless window, taking in the view of a three-story slum in Southeast Asia. Beneath the window, jutting through the walls of makeshift homes, plastic pipes carrying raw sewage could be seen spilling into a small tributary below. The slowly moving stream meandered through the slums where a secluded world of activity hosted a vibrant alternative economy that kept this area alive. The boy's face represented the youthful innocence contained within each of us, and the backdrop was a stark reminder of how hard some people have to fight just to survive.

This image highlighted something very basic about how we communicate. It told a rich story without a single word. Just as music transcends language to make spirits soar or bring deep peace to the soul, images can spark an entire narrative in the viewer that speaks directly to the human experience.

That, I think, is why we devote so much of our attention to today's digital media, and why I am so passionate about how we use and benefit from it. At its core, storytelling is much more elemental than using language to tell a tale. Stories—regardless of how they're told—are how we express ourselves to our friends, our families, and our communities. They reflect everything that makes us who we are and what we stand for.

A Storyteller's Perspective: The Engine of Imagination

Humans are storytelling animals. The creation of myths and legends seems to be a uniquely human trait. Other creatures can let it be known that there is danger nearby or food to be found, but they do not communicate about things that do not exist in the physical world—the ideas and beliefs born from the imagination, which help give meaning to human life and shape behavior, seem to belong only to Homo sapiens.

Indeed, the need to tell stories seems to be innate to all humans, a survival mechanism through which we understand our world, explain the past, process and manage the present, and imagine the future. Through stories we transmit values to our children and preserve and articulate our cultures. Stories help to give us some sense of control in our lives.

The cinematic takes us a step further than the literary or oral traditions in that it allows us to physically manipulate time and space and concretely visualize what we imagine. It has always been the filmmaker's struggle to put on the screen what he or she sees in the mind's eye. With only simple analog tools at their disposal, storytellers like Ray Harryhausen took us into space in the 1940s and Alfred Hitchcock terrified us with birds in the 1960s.

Today the digital power at our disposal allows us not only to make remarkable images and hear sounds that do not exist in the physical world, but also to spread these experiences globally at amazing speed, implanting these images and the ideas they convey in the minds of millions. The digital tools that enable us to create new kinds of narratives and share ideas bring an awesome responsibility as well as aesthetic and commercial potential.

As we know only too well from witnessing how contemporary terrorists exploit the Internet, media-makers can inspire both good and evil. It is unbelievably dangerous to underestimate the power of the cinematic stories that fill our multitude of screens and will soon come to us in the immersive environments of virtual and augmented reality—power to educate, to give pleasure, to transmit values, to inspire action.

"It's only entertainment" is perhaps the most frightening statement one can make about contemporary media. Cinema and her children—television, games, immersive environments—have the power to change human behavior and, therefore, to change our world.

—Elizabeth Daley, dean of the USC School of Cinematic Arts (SCA)

SHAPING OUR VIEW OF THE WORLD

Our stories form a foundation that can strengthen or weaken the social fabric, and as our stories evolve, so does the society we live in. They reflect, in part, the state of our evolution. They connect us to common issues; they allow us to move forward and adapt; they allow us to share ideas, to inspire, to educate. And that, in today's world, is why audio and visual media—and the way they are used to tell stories—matter so much. The way we interact with these media has a profound effect on our culture.

Recent history bears this out. The Vietnam War marked a turning point in American history, when the nation's attitudes toward armed conflict underwent a fundamental shift. It wasn't the fact that the war was costly in both blood and treasure—the country had experienced that before. No, the difference was that for the first time, there was an immediacy to the story. Images of what war was really like were seen by the public, with less filtering than had previously been presented.

This was no heroic, patriotic war movie or heavily edited newsreel. The grim reality of war was on television every night, and some of the most iconic photos of our time appeared in print—indelible images like the 1972 photo of Phan Thi Kim Phúc, the little girl running naked down a road after being burned in an American napalm attack, or South Vietnamese National Police Chief Nguyên Ngọc Loan summarily executing a Viet Cong prisoner by shooting him in the head.

Such raw stories also highlight the close ties between culture and the way those stories are told. The same events seen from the other side had a very different interpretation. Outside Ho Chi Minh City, there's a war museum where visitors can see the actual tunnels used by the Viet Cong, with exhibits that tell a very different story from the one familiar to U.S. citizens. These depictions may seem shocking and incomprehensible to Americans, but from the Vietnamese point of view, they are stories of heroism.

Aside from the many tragedies of war itself, the stories told by both sides reflect the geopolitical concerns of their respective communities and countries, the raw stories of actual battles allowing everyone to debate the worthiness of the sacrifices, the changing views of governance, and the roles sovereign states should have on what are perceived as common issues.

The Vietnam War experience shaped thinking on modern warfare and the effectiveness of modern weapons. It also brought an intense appreciation for the life-changing experiences that soldiers on both sides endured, that many had a hard time recovering from, and still more speak about to this day. These events didn't only spawn stories about a war; they reflect how we feel about war and our perspective on its futility and cost.

This was yet another example of the ongoing role of technology in allowing stories to be told from anywhere and consumed at any time. The first-person view of the Vietnam War continues to echo in our consciousness, affecting how the story of the news unfolds.

Today citizen journalism has torn down any natural filtering of raw video, allowing media companies to have nearly unlimited access to content that can better tell the story. It also has dramatically increased both the number of news outlets and the economic pressure to produce the best, most compelling story for any given event—and that often translates into a harsh, unblinking view of the world. The youthful innocence that was punctured by televised events like the Vietnam War is truly gone. We are now bombarded daily by powerful images of terrorist acts, police shootings, tragic accidents, and global atrocities.

A Storyteller's Perspective: Empowering the Citizen Correspondent

Traditional news media outlets used to have a direct and heavy impact on public opinion in the Arab world. Because of this, decision makers in the media industry didn't take emerging social media platforms seriously. But social media attracted Arab youth with unexpected speed and became a pivotal tool in the news.

Arab youth feel marginalized politically, socially, and economically; this ingrained belief is linked to traditional media outlets, which they believe left them behind.

In 2011, these disaffected young people fanned the flames of the "Arab Spring" that swept many countries and took to social media, fervently posting videos, releasing anti-regime articles and slogans on Twitter, Facebook, and YouTube. Since then, Arab youth have increasingly used another tool in planning and mobilizing support for their ideas—the mobile phone. Its ease of use allows the average person to shoot and post videos instantly. A new generation of communicators is in the midst of a successful, real-world experiment that has propelled social communication to a new level.

This put traditional Arab media outlets in a challenging situation in which they were incapable of keeping up with the advantages of "new media" tools. In response, they launched verified accounts on various social media platforms to compete with informal social media for breaking news. Thus, citizen storytellers have prompted traditional media to relinquish its arrogant attitude toward social media, and instead take advantage of it to relate news to viewers.

—Turki Aldakhil, general manager, Alarabiya & Alhadath news channels

---

GREAT STORIES TOUCH US DEEPLY, NO MATTER WHAT THE MEDIUM

At many of the exhibitions on my photo tour, the image of the boy in the slum and others like it provoked strong reactions. Most viewers reacted emotionally, and a few, even viscerally. Some felt tremendous compassion for the boy in the picture, while others were simply astonished to suddenly find themselves face-to-face with an image depicting such atrocious living conditions. Many felt an urge to help raise the boy's living standard and asked how they could help his family directly.

I found it remarkable that a photography exhibit highlighting the strength of the human spirit resulted in several deep conversations with donors who were so disturbed by what they saw that they were driven to passionately discuss their feelings. Many recognized the dichotomy of viewing such grim and discomforting images while sipping fine champagne and nibbling on specially made *hors d'oeuvres*.

What became clear was how engaged they were in the stories laid out before them—stories about communities around the world and the people living in them, each searching for a better way of life using whatever resources they had at their command. It was a stark reminder that humanity has always had a need to search for purpose and meaning, and that stories are the part of our social fabric that connects our fears, our hopes, and our dreams.

The human reactions I saw show just how powerful stories can be, even when told by nothing more than a single image. The same power to move people can be found in film, television, music, performance, visual and tactile arts, and written and spoken words. That's what's so marvelous about human communication—we can reach and touch one another in so many ways. And now we have amazing, unprecedented tools and resources available with which to express ourselves. Digitizing the joy of storytelling is opening up new vistas and empowering us like never before.

As the chairman and CEO of one of the largest media technology companies in the world, what I experienced at those exhibitions reinforces what we in the media industry have always known: storytelling is a key part of our human existence, as embedded in our DNA as anything else we do. The joyful urge to share, to enlighten, to inspire, and to delight is eternal. Only the methods change.

CHAPTER 2

Why Do We Do This?

There's always room for a story that can transport people to another place.

—J. K. Rowling

Ask a group of musicians why they learned to play, and you might expect to hear someone say, "To meet girls [or boys]." An actor might answer, "To become a star." A reporter might tell of wanting to become a prime-time network anchor. While fame, money, and the clichés of sex, drugs, chartered flights, and chauffeured cars may be part of what drives some, superficial trappings like these barely scratch the surface.

One of the biggest surprises I've encountered in my time in the media business has been how completely immersed the most successful people are in what they do. The truly talented artists, singers, actors, directors, musicians—and also editors, mixers, sound designers, coders, and technologists of all kinds—are completely in love with storytelling and how the tools of media enable it.

I often like to ask people in the industry why they think they are successful and what drove them to pursue a career in entertainment or media. In the vast majority of cases, it came from a very personal and emotional place that was about them sharing something powerful and of their own spirit in overcoming life's difficulties. The most rewarding aspect of being part of this industry is that so many of the most successful people are completely committed to connecting with communities for the right reasons.

The music side of media is a perfect example. Over the years I've met artists, writers, and producers from all over the world—from hard-core rappers to folks who focus on ballads and everything in between. No matter where I go, there's one thing that strikes me about all of them: they all talk the same way about what they do. Despite extreme differences—where they grew up, their family and cultural background, their life experiences, their current lives—they share a deep desire and powerful commitment to sharing their stories with others.

In my career I've probably visited every major media company in the world and interacted with professionals who play roles in every part of the media value chain. I've had the good fortune to be privy to the latest in cutting-edge viewing and immersive technology—media experiences that the public won't see for years. I've attended major award shows, sat in music studios with the biggest artists, and been on the sets of major broadcasters, studios of major film production companies, newsrooms, the largest live sporting events, and most recognized gaming development houses. From my perspective, most people on the creative side don't talk about "success." They speak instead of connecting with others, telling the best story, sharing experiences, honing their craft, finding the truth, delighting the audience, exciting the senses, and being heard.

Video editors, music mixers, gaming developers, and news producers are more concerned with telling the best story possible, one that captures the essence of the message, stirs the soul, and inspires the imagination. And for many behind the scenes, the glamour aspect doesn't come into play at all. Becoming part of the huge and diverse media ecosystem at any level and sticking with it inspires a deeper connection—a more powerful and meaningful motivation.

A Storyteller's Perspective:
We're All Storytellers

Storytelling, as we know it, has been around as long as there have been human beings. From the small child learning her first words to the retiree eager to share his tales, we are all inherent storytellers. We have always been that way, sharing knowledge, experience, learning, and excitement through the medium of narrative and character and setting.

Today, there are more opportunities than ever before to create and share stories, thanks to the power of technology. It has revolutionized our society. It has enabled us to reach bigger and broader audiences, while simultaneously giving us more creative flexibility in how we craft and distribute our stories. Technology in this day and age is more powerful than ever, and for the first time, it does not limit or define our stories; our imagination is the only limit.

If we don't have human beings engaged in our stories, then we have nothing at all. No matter what point in time we live in, storytelling will transcend all technology, and it's critical for us to always remember that. Powerful technologies are amplifiers and enablers. The essence is the human experience. Nothing else matters.

—Fred Mattocks, general manager, English Services Media Operations,
Canadian Broadcasting Corporation

THE URGE TO SHARE

On the content side, motivations are rooted in the same powerful feelings that spur creativity. An actor, filmmaker, or video game designer may be moved by the joy of crafting an imaginary world for characters to inhabit. A broadcast journalist might feel a deep sense of public duty and a devotion to truth. For a songwriter, it's often the desire to be heard—to make a statement that resonates emotionally, spiritually, or even politically. A performing musician or stage actor may thrive on the electricity of connecting with a live audience.

Storytelling is also about participation. Just as novels and short stories come to life only in the imagination of the reader, video games are collaborative stories created in part by the designers and in part by the players. Thriving global communities have sprung up around games like *World of Warcraft*, with millions of people taking part in the stories that they themselves create. There's a deep connection between those who designed that world and those who, in a very real sense, live there. With the advancement of immersive technologies, those worlds are only going to become more compelling.

Broadcast and online journalism are also becoming ever more participatory and immersive. News outlets embrace social media and interaction, encouraging submissions and commentary from viewers and allowing ordinary people to become part of the evolving story. It is now commonplace for TV news outlets to not only read live tweets on the air but report on a trending tweet as a story in itself. And with the majority of people carrying phones with connectivity and video capability, it's easier than ever to become part of the global news-gathering apparatus. No longer do reporters and camera crews have to rush to the scene of a breaking news story; witnesses and the participants themselves can take on much of that function, and they do so enthusiastically.

This trend toward citizen journalism speaks to the same deep human need that drives all storytellers—to communicate and share. It also changes the story itself, adding new dimensions and perspectives that contribute to, and often shape, the narrative. Many stories now become important parts of our cultural conversation largely because a person with a camera caught the event on video, changing public perceptions in the process. The citizen video of the 1991 Rodney King beating led directly to riots in Los Angeles the following year after the officers involved were acquitted. The 2014 choke-hold incident involving the death of Eric Garner sparked a wave of public interest in capturing news and holding police more accountable. We now live in a society where we become firsthand witnesses to (and often participants in) the story as it happens.

Crowd-sourcing coverage of events isn't limited to citizen contributors covering hard news. For live sporting events, there are apps that those in attendance can use to share the content they capture with the broadcaster. Imagine the power broadcasters have when they can go from 30 cameras to 40,000 and capture far more of what's happening both on the field and with the fans. Imagine the experience of having a virtual seat in the stadium with the freedom to look around as if you were actually there. The increase in ability to tell the best story and capture the intensity of the game is exponential, to say the least. It's an unprecedented ability to engage the audience in a much more intimate and powerful way—to deepen and pro-long the connection.

THE NEED TO SHAPE OUR COMMUNITY

Our stories often reflect the hopes, dreams, and concerns of a community. Concerns about war, the wonders of outer space, the need to understand, to deeply love and connect, and to find purpose and meaning are a reflection of the types of stories we tell. Following the Vietnam War, movies like *The Deer Hunter* and *Full Metal Jacket* helped the community address and process the painful experiences that many encountered and the questions those experiences generated.

Humans have always had a strong interest in what impacts everyone, from discussions of faith, safety, and living conditions to justice, equality, and significant events in the life of the community. The concerns of today are reflected in the stories we tell, just as they were when cave drawings educated people about food supplies or battles. In this way, the desire to share these stories and the increasing power to do it are intense drivers of the continued growth of the media industry.

The stories we tell shape how we feel and help us work through what's happening in the world around us. We see it in songs, literature, games, art, and film, both fiction and documentaries. Even our day-to-day interactions with those around us create a narrative that guides us and helps us understand both the events and the attitudes of others. The stories we tell, large and small, deep and trivial, serious and joking, all reflect what's happening—and there's a deep-seated human need to tell those stories. Look at any Facebook or Instagram feed and it's easy to see this in action.

Stories are both a product of what's happening in the society that created them and a means to influence that society. Without cultural and historical context, their true meaning is easily lost in translation. Myths, legends, performances, literature, film, and music from other cultures reflect those cultures and the events that impact them. It's hard enough to appreciate, or even understand, a story from another human culture—one can only imagine how lost we'd be if we were to encounter the stories of an alien race. This is why the motivation to create and share stories is universal; it's something that's essential to every human's cultural narrative.

Storytelling is also a tool that can have specific purpose. Increasingly, governments and other interest groups are gaining an appreciation for the power of social dialogue. We've seen more active engagement by sovereign states, public and private organizations, and individuals as a way to influence people and shape public opinion. Indeed state-controlled media can be a very powerful tool within a country's borders, shielded from outside influence. In more open societies, government funding of media channels can protect them from market forces, thus increasing their influence.

In America, which many around the world see as a beacon of freedom, free speech, and free thinking, ostensibly neutral media outlets are increasingly shaped by editorial bias and the clearly stated views of their audiences. This evident bias in mainstream media pales in comparison to digital-only platforms that barely disguise their one-sided views—if indeed they even try to portray themselves as unbiased.

A Storyteller's Perspective: Finding the Voice of the People

Sometimes, to find your voice, you need to balance your own against that of others. In that sense, only through the Internet have people been able to find an audience for what they have to say. It helps you learn from and collaborate with others, fine-tune your point of view, and ultimately end up defining exactly who you are and what you are about to become a voice that is heard.

Since its inception in 1996, the Al Jazeera Media Network has sought to be the voice of the voiceless. We wanted to become a platform that echoes the voice of the people, allowing similar and opposing opinions to have a voice, where viewers are the judges of what side they want to be a part of.

In our experience, prior to the creation of Al Jazeera, state-sponsored media was pretty much the only voice in the Middle East. Having a player come in that was editorially independent allowed people to speak their minds. Without technological innovations, we would not have the ability to push these independent messages and allow people to be able to choose what side they want to take on a given issue.

It is no longer a one-way message in which we project what we, or our guests, think, and people have to listen to it without responding. Now, it is a completely interactive relationship with a high level of engagement. We know if people like it, dislike it, are sharing it, or have viewed it. During our programs, people can interact in real time by sending tweets, and our presenters can tweet back or answer their queries within the live broadcast. The relationship between the creator and the consumer has transformed, which helps people from disparate places with different backgrounds and diverse points of view collaborate.

For Al Jazeera, we wanted to change the tone of the conversation. Technological solutions that enable us to have bidirectional relationships have made a big difference because now we can hear what people are thinking. That has opened the door to many who were previously on the periphery to come in and participate.

—Mohamed Abuagla, executive director of technology & operations (CIO/CTO) at Al Jazeera Media Network

In the push to build consensus and promote particular points of view, more stories are being used to shape our collective views. This is an era in which tools to communicate openly are more prevalent than ever. The public forum has more and more agenda-driven constituents, both government-supported and independent, taking advantage of this increased access to communities around the world. There's been a proliferation in investment by sovereign states and governments to ensure that their voice is heard globally by creating a way for them to tell their stories from their perspective. Other special-interest groups have also used greater connectivity to build consensus around their views. Finding news sources that are truly independent is getting harder and harder; in some instances, it's necessary to look to other countries to get a different perspective on current events.

THE REWARDS OF MAKING IT REAL

Those who support content creators get involved and stay engaged for their own reasons, often just as driven by emotion as the most passionate artist or visionary. For a sound-mix engineer, it might be taking pleasure in molding a recording artist's sound. A television producer or news editor

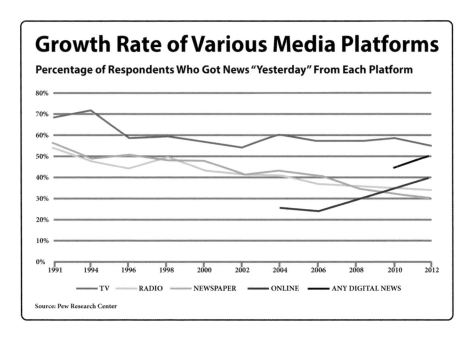

Growth Rate of Various Media Platforms

Percentage of Respondents Who Got News "Yesterday" From Each Platform

Source: Pew Research Center

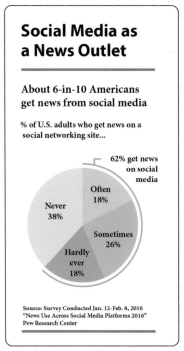

Social Media as a News Outlet

About 6-in-10 Americans get news from social media

% of U.S. adults who get news on a social networking site...

62% get news on social media

Often 18%

Never 38%

Sometimes 26%

Hardly ever 18%

Source: Survey Conducted Jan. 12-Feb. 8, 2016
"News Use Across Social Media Platforms 2016"
Pew Research Center

More people than ever are turning to digital sources for news. Often, these sources are unfiltered, making them a powerful tool for influencing opinion.

may find deep satisfaction and fulfillment of a sense of duty in bringing something new and meaningful into people's living rooms. For an A&R exec (a vanishing breed these days) or actor's agent, it could be the excitement of discovery and the warm feeling of mentoring someone who goes on to great success.

Even those at the other end of the chain—the fans—bring their own passion and make real contributions. Back in the day, they did so by buying records, going to movies, and tuning in to television broadcasts by the millions. In a digital world, they can play an expanded role by sharing new discoveries on social media and giving instant feedback to artists that can shape content, making them co-creators of the story itself. Some even become influential tastemakers in their own right by blogging about new music, TV, films, and games.

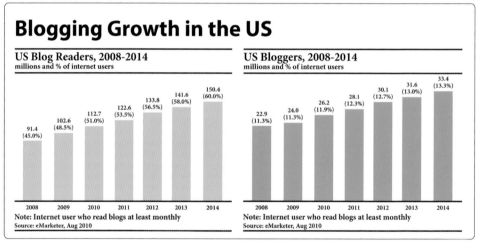

In the digital age, anyone with an Internet connection can use the power of storytelling to shape community opinion without having to pass through the filter of traditional media. More and more people are taking advantage of these outlets . . . and more are listening to what they have to say.

WE'RE ALL ON A SHARED JOURNEY

Every link in the media chain, from the creative minds that generate content to the final consumers who drive demand, is vitally important. But this connection between the storyteller and the consumer has become much more complicated. It's become more formalized and even industrialized.

Over time, oral traditions in which stories were told, then retold and passed down through generations from person to person began to give way to a more complex, longer chain with the storyteller at one end and the audience at the other.

As society developed, storytelling in all its forms became more of a profession, and new, specialized roles sprang up to support the storyteller and the process. It probably started with writing that allowed stories to live outside the memory of the storyteller—an added layer that involved the creation of a medium to preserve the story and a skilled person to record it. Whole new trades sprang up: publishers, booksellers, dedicated news correspondents, traveling acting troupes, composers making their living by creating commissioned works for royalty or wealthy patrons, and professional musicians to perform those works who were supported by professional instrument makers. The chain became longer still.

Along the way, technology has been part of the evolution, adding more complexity. For example, scribes gave way to printing presses, with specialists to operate them and a distribution system to get stories into the hands of consumers.

The dawn of the twentieth century accelerated this process, with increased connectivity and access to storytelling. Broadcasting and mass media in the form of film and newspapers—all the direct result of technology—changed the way stories were told and consumed. The media industry was born, growing to become a major economic force. As it evolved, the whole process of storytelling changed; steps in the workflow, from creation to consumption, were grouped and made scalable, ultimately becoming more automated. That took more specialized participants. The chain between storyteller and audience became still longer.

Today there's another metamorphosis taking place, driven by digital tools that facilitate content creation and new channels that connect storytellers to audiences. Supporting this expansion is the fact that many of the traditional steps in the media workflow have been automated and connected through technology. With the advent of a fully digital workflow, everyone can adapt to the new realities without undermining what works. But even as the individual steps become more automated and connected, they also proliferate due to new demands imposed by technology; there are more platforms, more channels, more file formats, and more business models to get stories to the consumer. As a result, there is growing complexity in the whole process.

A Storyteller's Perspective: Technology and the Craft of Storytelling

The art of storytelling and the technology available have always been intrinsically linked. With the rise of video and the ever-increasing power of digital tools, we're in a new golden age of content not seen since the early days of television. The craft of editing and media management no longer have the complexity they used to, allowing creators to produce diverse content with ease.

Although web-based distribution methods have undoubtedly shaken traditional broadcasters to the core, they also have given unprecedented freedom of choice to the consumer. This choice has helped creative video production flourish and meet the needs of an increasingly diverse viewership.

YouTube provides an example in which the human need to share stories is given an outlet. Certainly, YouTube has become a distribution platform in its own right, but it's also become an entry point into mainstream broadcasting as new talent is discovered and promoted. TVNZ's on-demand service now carries short-form drama created within this burgeoning creative community, showcasing the work of this new talent.

These new platforms put the power of creativity back in to the hands of the creators to unlock endless content possibilities. Truly, a new paradigm in content creation has been reached.

—Lindsay Chalmers, general manager of enterprise operations,
Television New Zealand (TVNZ)

And yet, even as the chain that links storytellers to their audiences becomes longer and more complicated, the basic need to connect with one another remains. Each link in the chain matters. You may be an amateur with a webcam posting a video to YouTube, you could be a rising star gaining a following online, you may be a master of production adept in the latest tools, or you might be a hotshot media mogul. No matter where you fit into the picture, you're a valuable part of what makes the vast media landscape so amazing.

It's the desire to be part of that shared experience that captivates us and keeps us engaged. Think about your own motivations. Life is busier than ever, with more demands, with more responsibilities, and the pace of change is accelerating. And yet, despite more and more demands on our time, there is a significant increase in consumption patterns for rich media. In the past ten years alone, media consumption has increased by almost 50 percent. What else in your life has increased by 50 percent in the past ten years? The list must be small. So why are we devoting more time to media consumption?

Because storytelling speaks to us, and we want to be part of it. Because connecting with one another through stories that move us matters, whether it's for learning or inspiration. Because we want to share the joy that storytelling brings to all of us.

The Olympics: Inspiration on a Global Scale

I was in Rio for the 2016 Summer Olympics and saw firsthand the incredible dedication to telling stories that media professionals from all over the world brought to the event. Many of them lived on-site for over a year in an intense, stress-filled environment, just to feel the joy and satisfaction of getting the story of the games to audiences in their communities back home. Pride in their accomplishments and in the efforts of their nations' athletes were on display everywhere, from the huge cadres of professionals from countries like the United States to tiny but intensely patriotic teams from countries like Cuba.

For these technical and creative professionals, the personal sacrifice of being away from their families, with grueling hours working in a small workspace shoulder to shoulder with thousands in a foreign country, was inspiring and deeply moving.

It's this ability to become part of the storytelling process by more in the community that is having a fundamental impact on media. Not just in regard to the level of engagement, number of stories, and number of ways to connect—it's redefining the economics of the industry itself and causing everyone involved to stop and reevaluate their roles.

CHAPTER 3

Our Roles Are Changing— and Expanding

I've a feeling we're not in Kansas anymore.
—From *The Wizard of Oz*

It's a very exciting time in the media industry, because more people than ever have access to powerful creative and production tools and the means to share with others. We are all tremendously empowered as a result.

In a scant few years the world has changed radically, opening up access to the best technology available. Software and hardware that once cost a small fortune and required days or weeks of training to use are now easy to obtain by just about anyone. Buy a new laptop today, and it will come with free software that would have made a seasoned professional's jaw drop a few decades ago. There are even studio-quality tools that run on smartphones and tablets.

As an example, Pro Tools—by far the most popular music-creation program used by professional media artists and music, film, and broadcast studios all over the world—now has a free version available to anyone. You can remotely connect via the cloud to other artists, composers, and directors and work as though you were in the same room via video chat. Now you can work with the best, anywhere at any time. Content creation, production, and distribution technologies have become so simple and ubiquitous that almost anyone with a story to tell now has the power to tell it in a compelling way.

A Storyteller's Perspective: Creativity and the Power of Technology

When I first started recording music as a teenager, the barrier for entry was very high. The first recording hardware I bought was right around 1986. I got a Tascam 388 reel-to-reel, all-in-one tape-recorder unit. My parents had to take out a loan in order to buy the machine, which was around $3,000. Throw in guitars, keyboards, drum machines, and other music equipment, and my investment ballooned up to around $7,000, or about $12,000 in today's money.

That's a lot for a kid working at a music store. Every cent I made went back into creating my first studio.

Nowadays, it's much easier to go from a musical idea that only exists in your head to getting it recorded. I'll start by jotting down ideas, grabbing an acoustic guitar, and recording a voice memo onto my phone. I can then take that phone recording and plug it into any number of programs. What once required a huge investment in several pieces of hardware can be done on one single program, on a tiny interface that can fit in your backpack. You can be on your computer recording songs and send them across the world on Dropbox or in the new Pro Tools 12 and collaborate over the cloud.

Sometimes I think the endless options created by modern software can slow creativity a bit. With newer technology, I find myself looking through pages and pages of loops or sounds when the focus should really be on creating first. But it's also great to have that problem. The fact that you're able to collaborate with musicians now over the Internet is a huge breakthrough in recording. As it gets better, it'll be like you're in the studio together even if you're working across an ocean.

It's a really exciting time in music. It's taken what seemed unattainable for the casual musician into something that can be created on a small budget at their leisure, instead of booking studio time or buying expensive equipment. The quality you can get for minimal cost is pretty amazing.

—Paul Sidoti, professional musician

Because even our most advanced tools have become so inexpensive and easy to use, more storytellers have the ability to compose and record a song, create a film, publish a book, or make an immersive video game experience with professional results.

But it's not only the creative tools that have changed. The resources, processes, and services that enable production and distribution have also gotten much more sophisticated and lower-priced. That's changing the fundamentals of the media ecosystem, thanks in large part to the unprecedented level of connectedness that has become part of everyday life.

No longer does a person need to be a media professional to share his or her experiences and views with the world. Shoot a video, and the entire process of editing, adding a sound track, and globally distributing it digitally can be accomplished in a few hours at home, without the help of trained experts. That story can be seen by billions the same day it's created. What an incredibly compelling idea that is! And if you are not a professional, your work can be included in a professional workflow (with proper permissions) much more easily than just a few years ago, marking the continued evolution of the connection between the creative process and the audience.

For professionals in the media sector, these same advances in technology and connectivity are causing even the most proven models to change. As the industry evolved over decades, steps in the media workflow became more clearly defined and automated to allow a systematic approach to storytelling and distribution.

Today, advances in technology are disrupting every aspect of this media value chain and causing large media organizations to rethink their role in the media ecosystem as they work to remain relevant. The digitization of the connection between the creative process and consumer is causing a fundamental reevaluation of the processes themselves, and economic realities are accelerating the pressure to change the status quo.

This is providing a moment of clarity for everyone involved and raising some fundamental questions: What is my place in the media value chain and what value do I bring? Why am I here and why do I matter?

A Storyteller's Perspective: Technology Has Changed Our Role—But It Hasn't Changed Storytelling

Twenty-five years ago, I became the first person to edit a studio feature film with Avid Media Composer: Lost in Yonkers. *In the years that followed, as I worked with Avid to help design these tools, my peers and I came to believe that digital editing would make our lives dramatically easier. The mundane, organizational parts of our jobs would be handled by computers, and we'd be free to focus on the work we enjoyed most: putting images and sounds together into coherent narratives.*

How naïve that sounds today. Digital editing has certainly made it easier to organize, access, and experiment with video and audio. But as our tools got better, our responsibilities expanded. The result, a quarter of a century later, is that our work is far more technically demanding, and our workload has only increased.

The digital revolution eventually transformed not only post production but also acquisition and distribution. The resulting changes have been similarly unexpected. When DVRs first made their appearance, networks saw them as an existential threat. When streaming services arrived, they were likewise seen as business-model killers. Instead, we are now experiencing a golden age of dramatic television, with so many new, high-quality shows that some wonder if the market is overcrowded.

The digital media revolution is nothing if not a humbling lesson in unintended consequences. We're good at building tools but not nearly so good at predicting their effects. Meanwhile, despite these tectonic changes, the fundamental skills needed to construct a story have remained surprisingly consistent. Whether we edit with a razor blade or a mouse, we evaluate and build material using the same mental and emotional constructs.

We've moved from cave paintings to Jumbotrons, from smoke signals to fiber optics and LTE, but the shape and structure of our narratives, and the underlying urge to create and experience them, hasn't changed. I've spent a good part of my life helping to design tools for artists. The tools evolve, the artists adapt, but the underlying stories endure.

—Steven Cohen, A.C.E. editor: *Bosch, The Bridge, 15 Minutes*

Connectivity is a critically important part of these shifts. The Internet and mobile technologies have done nothing less than create billions of participants in a vibrant global dialogue, each empowered by a platform that lets them reach the whole world. You can quickly locate and connect with like-minded people and be part of any affinity group with unprecedented ease, whenever you like, no matter where in the world they may be. If you have an interest in anything at all, no matter how obscure, you can immediately connect with others who share the same interests—a community without borders. The sheer scope of this online universe is far removed from everyday experience, as is the ceaseless activity that takes place. With nearly 1.1 billion users,[1] if Facebook were a country, it would be the third largest in the world.[2] Every day, more than 500 million tweets get sent,[3] while Instagram photo and video shares have grown to more than 95 million per day.[4]

Each year, the company I lead holds an industry conference called Avid Connect that brings this sense of dynamic global community vividly to life. Leading professionals from the largest media companies fly in from all around the world to compare notes on the state of the industry. Picture a massive room full of media industry leaders from more than fifty countries around the world, representing the nearly 10,000 member organizations that make up the Avid Customer Association. These are the passionate storytellers who distribute the most popular shows and the most compelling live sporting events; they create the best television programs, and they represent the most recognized brands in news, film, scripted shows, sports, and gaming. It is a very humbling experience.

More importantly, I am constantly amazed by the camaraderie, enduring spirit of innovation, and the deep engagement, commitment, and enthusiasm of Avid Connect attendees. It is abundantly clear to me how much what we do matters, and we are so excited about the endless possibilities it helps create for all. It is equally clear that the industry, comprising all the myriad parts played by everyone involved, continues to accelerate at a rate that shows no signs of slowing. That same energy can be found at similar events held by companies, industry organizations, and special interest groups all over the world.

FOR THE INDUSTRY, TECHNOLOGY IS DISRUPTIVE

As empowering as innovations in technology and communications have been on the individual level, they've also led to the creation of a massive and poorly balanced industrial juggernaut with technology at its center. Even as new tools and channels offered easier creation and access to distribution for the storyteller, they also led to complexity on a huge scale that has resulted in serious and ongoing issues not only for the media industry and its participants but for the community at large.

Gone are the days of simple, predictable economic models that can be scaled and repeated. The company I run was founded nearly thirty years ago with a mission to re-imagine storytelling. That year, what was to become one of the most iconic shows in television history, *Seinfeld*, was launched to critical acclaim; though it started slowly, within a few years it was leading the Nielsen ratings and had become something of a cultural phenomenon. For most of the population, unless you recorded it on your VCR, you had to watch it on that special night that it was broadcast. That mattered because it was so popular: if you didn't, you wouldn't be able to talk about the show the next morning at the office. You'd miss out on the social interaction around the story: until you were able to catch the episode as a rerun or in syndication, the stories that were told would simply be office legend about this popular show that was about "nothing."

Back then there was no way to watch episodes on demand, as is common today. Distribution was very limited and the economic model was simpler. The entire season would certainly not be available until it eventually came out on VHS long after the initial broadcast, and there was of course no Internet or mobile access.

Today the consumption and economic models have changed dramatically, becoming much more complex and unpredictable. Take the product placements, consumer brand tie-ins, and co-marketing agreements with retailers that are now commonplace as an example. They were once rare and often debated. Now, there may be marketing campaigns coordinated with consumer brands. Entire seasons might be launched on digital channels only or concurrently with broadcast. Seasons may be released all at once. There could be second-screen interactive tools, extended online content, and on and on. Beyond the major digital platforms, cable, or broadcast networks, even more creative launch and revenue-generation practices are constantly cropping up.

Similar linkages happen in the world of film. Long before an eagerly anticipated blockbuster hits the multiplex, the marketing engine revs up. We see tie-ins with everything from fast food to car insurance, not to mention massive merchandising and licensing efforts. All of this activity is a significant revenue driver, and all of it sits on top of the actual production. There are also supplemental productions that generate buzz, from teaser videos to multiple trailers available only online, and PR campaigns to product-specific websites. It's a far cry from the "coming soon" posters that used to appear at the local cinema.

There's another phenomenon that's having a significant impact on the box office. Because of social media, audience engagement plays a much larger role in a film's success. Relying on critic reviews in the Sunday paper is no longer the only way to tell if a movie is worth watching. Websites like rottentomatoes.com deliver audience consensus to us in near-real time; a film's success or failure can be decided even before it has a chance to build momentum.

About the same time that *Seinfeld* was launched, the movie that won the Academy Award for Best Edited Film was *Who Framed Roger Rabbit?* This too followed a fairly predictable economic model. At the time, the path for a major motion film would typically begin with a U.S. theater release, then an international release, premium cable TV distribution, and finally the local video rental store. Of course, back then, you would hope that they had it in stock and that you remembered to return it on time to avoid late fees. Many of us remember taking that late drive to the video store and leaving the car running while we sprinted to drop the tape in the return slot.

WHAT'S REALLY DRIVING DISRUPTION

The underlying story of industry disruption is rooted not in changing economic models but in the changes to the value chain that sits behind those models. Early on in the evolution of the media industry, the creative side and the monetization or business end became separated from one another. Processes were grouped to enjoy economies of scale in areas such as live production, film processing, editing and post production, mastering, duplication, and distribution. Then technology was added to bring more efficiency to each step in the process. In the intense search for greater efficiency, the industry moved to simpler and more ubiquitous tools. This worked well, as long as the economic models remained simple and well defined.

Now, we find that the changes in the media value chain are driving a complete reevaluation of the connection between those at either end: the storyteller and the consumer. In between are hundreds of vendors, processes, departments, and organizational constraints, isolating these two groups from one another. But it doesn't have to be this way.

Digitization changes the context. The connection from content creator to audience has reached the point where it can be entirely digitized. If we were to start from scratch and chart out how we'd like the person who creates the story and the person who consumes it to connect, we would create a very different link, one that is much more direct and simple, one that is more efficient and one that is much more immediate. And yet, every day the industry tries to reconcile the new reality with the old procedural constraints.

Media companies are struggling to make this happen even now. The fusion of the creative process with distribution and consumption—the advances in technology and greater engagement with the consumer—have led to an intense and dramatic change in the industry's view of how best to operate. It's also created a new challenge, especially for music companies; with creation and distribution so much more accessible to talented artists, music companies have a harder time justifying their role beyond marketing, promotion, and rights management.

A MATTER OF PRIORITIES: IT'S ABOUT MONEY

Earlier, I mentioned the rapid changes occurring in the media value chain. Chief among these is the disproportionate allocation of resources to running the system and monetizing its output, rather than creating the content on which it depends. The pressure on media companies today is as much about maximizing the economic value of media assets as it is about maximizing quality, but that's not simply because they are chasing profits. It's because they have to ensure that they are able to sustain their role in the industry. Many of the most successful media companies and professionals are making adjustments to not only survive changes to the economic model driving the industry but to emerge better able to serve their communities.

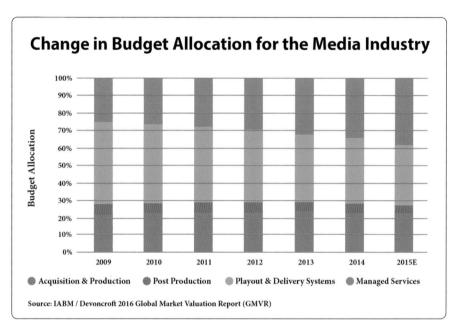

Change in Budget Allocation for the Media Industry

● Acquisition & Production ● Post Production ● Playout & Delivery Systems ● Managed Services

Source: IABM / Devoncroft 2016 Global Market Valuation Report (GMVR)

As complexity has increased in the new media ecosystem, companies are devoting more resources to managed services, while spending in traditional production and postproduction workflows has leveled off. According to a report by the International Association of Broadcasting Manufacturers and Devoncroft Partners, spending in the acquisition, production, and postproduction segments grew from $4.9 billion in 2009 to an estimated $5.6 billion in 2015, representing a 2 percent CAGR (compound annual growth rate). Over the same period, managed services grew from $4.4 billion to an estimated $7.7 billion, a 10 percent CAGR.[5]

A key driver of these changes is the relentless need to compete in a digital world. While the tools that are needed to tell stories have become more powerful and more accessible to storytellers (a good thing), the work required to transform the content for distribution has become exponentially more complex. The industry as a whole has had to expand critical work-streams in order to accommodate new technologies and channels, but it is hesitant to dismantle the more established part of the workflow.

This approach adds more cost and complexity, but the media industry is moving so fast that the perception is that there isn't time or money to reinvent the entire workflow, even though it's increasingly disjointed and inefficient. More activity means more cost, and that's pulling resources away from content creation.

An example of how expanding roles and complexity impact the industry (and cause an imbalance in resource allocation) is the huge increase in global distribution outlets, each with its own specific technical requirements. Where ten years ago, a broadcast network might make one "master" version of a TV program, today it needs to create hundreds of permutations of the program in different technical formats, containing variations in content for different audiences. Tailoring content for different audiences and transforming it into all the necessary formats has become an unwieldy, expensive, and inefficient process.

This imbalance is largely the result of the pace of innovation. New capabilities are coming online so fast that the business models, governing institutions, and social structures that have served well for many years are stretched and in danger of becoming obsolete.

As digitization accelerates and opens up new ways for people to share their creativity and consume content, media companies and professional content creators face a crisis. The economic shifts are moving faster than the industry's ability to adapt and expand on its traditional role. Historically limited distribution models and predictable financial models for various forms of content are changing quickly, which makes for a complicated environment that's hard for established media companies to navigate. They must cope with heritage infrastructure and reliance on declining revenue streams as they respond to the pressure to create the best content and combat new competitors that are free of the legacy burden. Actually making money—which is what keeps the content flowing—is becoming harder and harder for everyone, even as the amount of content explodes. In this new environment, who makes money and how they make it is changing rapidly.

A Storyteller's Perspective: The Increasing Difficulty of Monetizing Creativity

While technology makes it easier for artists to create and be heard, there's a direct link between this technology and how hard it is to reap the full benefits of whatever the artist creates.

The old compensation model has been blown up. Traditionally, artists relied on labels to fund their work. The artists then saw returns through the sale of vinyl, CDs, or downloads, while labels recouped the investment they had made. In that scenario, at least ideally, everyone wins.

For most artists, that model no longer exists. Even to book studio time— and we're not talking LA or New York—top recording studios charge anywhere from $600 to $1,300 a day. The average professional musician in the U.S. right now makes an average of $34,455 from music-specific gigs. That math doesn't *work. Even working on the side, you can't afford to pay a music studio $1,000 a day for, say, three weeks of studio time to record an album. And that's just a conservative estimate.*

We have to find another model. Increasingly, artists resort to do-it-yourself methods. Either they find a much smaller studio, or they do it themselves on a laptop or iPad. To do it yourself, you have to have a certain level of knowledge, and you have to have the tools.

And that's just the creation process. Once you create your product, you need to not just be heard but also make a living. As artists tour more because they make almost nothing from streaming and the number of CDs sold plummets through the floor, a lot of them struggle with how to monetize that one-shot deal of a live show, beyond YouTube, where they also make no money.

Technology for managing, sharing, and monetizing performances holds the promise to go beyond in-person attendance or live-streaming of a show, enabling artists to make money from that one event again and again. Once that code is cracked, the artist really has available a global audience that does not need to be eyeballs-to-screen when the concert takes place. As these tools evolve, so too will an artist's ability to make money off of her or his creation.

—Paula Boggs, musician

THE DIZZYING RATE OF CHANGE

The inability to keep up with the times is due in large part to the increasing pace of technological advancement that digitization makes possible.

It probably took our ancestors more than 100,000 years to go from inventing language to writing words down, but it took fewer than 7,000 years to go from the oldest known writing to the first printed page, and fewer than 600 years to progress from Gutenberg's printing press to the World Wide Web. But in the relatively few years since the world went online, the rate of change has exploded, outstripping the ability of many organizations and individuals to adapt fast enough to seize the new opportunities open to them.

Now we're tapping into a constantly changing 24/7 news feed on our phones, catching up with old friends on Facebook, watching our favorite television shows on Hulu, and wondering what comes next. We're constantly bombarded by innovations, from the latest apps and hardware to new social media platforms. "This year's model" is rapidly losing its meaning as product cycles get ever shorter.

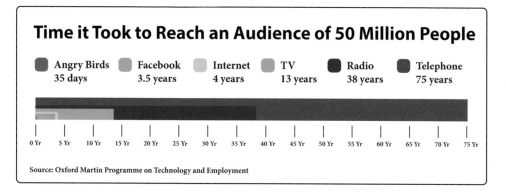

Time it Took to Reach an Audience of 50 Million People

- **Angry Birds** 35 days
- **Facebook** 3.5 years
- **Internet** 4 years
- **TV** 13 years
- **Radio** 38 years
- **Telephone** 75 years

Source: Oxford Martin Programme on Technology and Employment

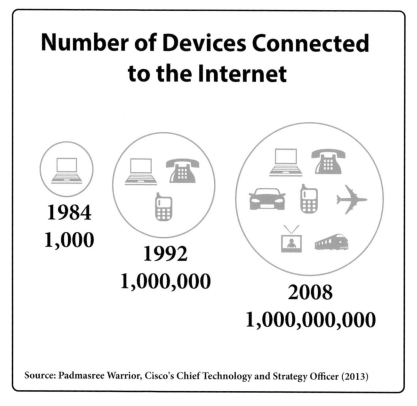

Number of Devices Connected to the Internet

1984
1,000

1992
1,000,000

2008
1,000,000,000

Source: Padmasree Warrior, Cisco's Chief Technology and Strategy Officer (2013)

This rapid acceleration is due to a simple principle: non-biological evolution doesn't have to be gradual. A game-changing idea can take root and spread across the planet with blazing speed, taking whole industries and societies off guard.

We live in an age in which it seems that virtually anything is possible, and the world can change overnight. For some, it seems that there's no time to reflect, absorb, and think about how the world is changing. Attention deficit is part of life today. Events, celebrities, and trends come and go and barely leave a ripple on the social consciousness because attention has turned to the next thing. We've grown so accustomed to rapid change that when it happens, we take it in stride and just chalk it up to Moore's law. It's all too easy to forget that hardly anyone has been using the Internet for much longer than twenty years.

Moore's Law

In 1965, Intel co-founder Gordon Moore wrote an article in which he observed that the number of transistors in integrated circuits had been doubling each year, predicting that the trend would continue for at least a decade. In 1975, he revised his projection to doubling every two years, but the trend was still intact.

Only now, fifty years later, are the laws of physics catching up and slowing the advance. Think about the last laptop you purchased; it probably isn't all that different in terms of performance from one you could buy five or even ten years ago. But throughout the 1980s and 1990s, speed and capacity were increasing by leaps and bounds almost on a yearly basis. We're reaching a physical limit, and engineers are now looking to quantum computing as the next engine of advancement.

Nevertheless, Moore's Law has proven remarkably durable, and in many ways the pace of change has accelerated. Thanks to end-run strategies, like the shift from disk drives to solid-state storage, and new computing strategies, like virtualization and in-memory processing, we're still seeing dramatic increases in capacity, even as the physical limits of the silicon chip get closer.

While Moore didn't speak to economics at the time, Moore's law is often understood to mean that real consumer prices actually fall as electronics get better. The socioeconomic effect of this has been enormous, with much of the productivity and economic growth of the latter part of the twentieth century attributable to the phenomenon.

What's interesting about Moore's Law is its side effects. As electronics get faster, smaller, and cheaper, new ways of doing things quite literally change the world around us. It's hard to find a single aspect of modern life that is not affected in some way by pervasive technology. Had prices remained high—or increased—with the advances in technology, our society would be very different.

The world is changing in astonishing ways because of this. Jobs like social media strategist, user experience designer, big data architect, cloud services specialist, and digital marketing specialist were almost unknown a decade ago . . . if they existed at all.[6] Today's students are preparing for jobs that will use technologies yet to be invented—and they'll be solving problems that, today, aren't even recognized as such.

According to Nielsen Online, as recently as September 2008, Google processed 4.8 billion search queries per month.[7] And according to Amit Singhal, SVP of search at Google, as of October 2015 that number has grown to more than 100 billion searches a month.[8]

The first text message was sent in 1992. Now, the number of texts sent each day exceeds the population of the whole world. And according to IBM, we generate 2.5 quintillion bytes (2.5×10^{18}) of data every day which means 90 percent of the data in the world today has been created in the last two years.[9]

The pace of change is forcing us to become more agile. According to the U.S. Bureau of Labor Statistics, young adults born in the early 1980s held an average of 7.2 jobs from age 18 through 28.[10] One in five workers have been with their current employer less than a year, and half have held their jobs for less than five years.[11]

Differentiating on Creativity

In the space of a few decades, our economic base has moved from manufacturing to services, then to knowledge. The physical is giving way to the digital, and increasingly, people have the opportunity to learn and compete anywhere. That's a world-changing phenomenon.

Why? Because it opens the door to a new way for individuals to compete. Creativity and ingenuity will distinguish one person from the next. Just as digitization allows content to be tailored to match the individual, the role people play in the economic engine will depend on their unique skills. Those who are more adaptable, creative, agile, and solutions-oriented will excel in this new environment.

What does this digital acceleration mean for those involved in media? Simply that the roles, processes, business models, and consumption patterns that seem to be fixed are anything but. Whole industries can face existential threats that seem to come from nowhere, such as "over the top" content providers like Netflix making it possible to bypass familiar video consumption models, or VoIP providers like Skype making the very idea of long-distance telephone calls archaic.

A Storyteller's Perspective: Sink or Swim— We Need to Get with the Program

Telling stories has never been more complex than it is today. Although the rules of storytelling are more or less the same as they were when our ancestors were painting on the walls of caves or passing them down by spoken word, the tools we use are in a constant state of change. If our ancestors were limited by the crude tools of their times, today what we can accomplish as artists is limited only by our imaginations.

The tools have progressed in their capabilities in ways I don't think I could have imagined thirty years ago when I began my career as an editor. Looking back through the various waves of change our industry has gone through, I often wonder how I managed to stay afloat in the ever-pounding oceans of change. The simple answer is that early on in my career, I made a commitment to learning new skills, and I embraced each new change head on as it arrived.

Technology has a tendency to grow and expand at ever-increasing speeds. Staying on top of new trends requires perseverance and determination. I am reminded of a friend who, shortly after the film industry transitioned away from cutting film, once said, "I am an analog man in a digital word!" Like many of us, the onset of changing technologies was daunting for my friend, but years later it became even more difficult for this person to compete as the rapid pace of change compounded and made it even harder to play catch-up. As I find myself aging, things that were once easy to pick up become slower to absorb.

Many of the tools that are available for the modern storyteller are so complex that they can take months or even years to learn proficiently. A solid foundation of knowledge is often the secret ingredient to being able to leverage new tools and techniques as we age. While it may be harder for me to learn new things as I get older, it's not impossible; it comes down to attitude and the application of consistent hard work. Of course it helps when you love what you do!

—Alan Edward Bell, A.C.E.

IS DIGITAL ACCELERATION A BURDEN OR A BENEFIT?

There's a generational aspect to the acceptance of change and the ability to shift roles. In a 2010 NPR interview, the late writer Nora Ephron (*Sleepless in Seattle, When Harry Met Sally*) said, "I think when you get older, things come along that you know are a test in some way of your ability to stay with it. And when e-mail came along, I was just going to fall in *love* with it. And I did. I can't believe it now—it's like one of those ex-husbands that you think, 'What was I *thinking*?' The point is that you can kind of keep up for a while and then, suddenly, something comes along and you think, 'I give up. I am never going to tweet. I'm just never going to.'"

This resistance is understandable. In the many speeches I've given about technology, I've often discussed the benefits and drawbacks of a more digitized existence. Grocery shopping can be held up as an example of how the digitization of a human activity could detract from an important time that a mother and her child may spend together—or it could be an opportunity to become closer. Is the role of the parent to provide (shop), to mentor (interact), or both? The obvious answer is "both," but what's the right balance? Technology is making that question a meaningful one.

The trip to the grocery store is often romanticized; it's filled with memories of a time to connect, a time to bond through the pursuit of a common goal, a time to participate in the life of the community. Grocery shopping with my mother certainly carries memories for me. Looking for the right items, seeing how we prepared for the meals, and comparing prices and ingredients—it was definitely something that was shared and remembered.

Some would argue that the fact that grocery shopping can now be completed in five minutes online or with a mobile device, with the food delivered straight to your door, is an example of how digitization isn't really connecting us. It's actually moving us further apart—shifting the roles we play. The counterargument is that if the parent had an hour to both go shopping and spend time with her child, instead of using the full hour on grocery shopping, the parent could spend five minutes online ordering groceries via smartphone and the other fifty-five minutes in more meaningful engagement with the child.

Maybe as importantly, that online order could predict future buying behaviors, offer incentives to save money, and present targeted offers that made the buying experience better; it could be tied in to the inventory management system of the store to more efficiently predict inventory levels. The result would be that the store, and the whole shopping experience, runs smoother and more efficiently, leaving more time and attention for that all-important personal interaction. Rather than being a burden or negative influence on the parenting role, new technology becomes a benefit—provided we see the potential and take advantage of it.

Companies like Foodie in Finland show this positive promise of technology in action. This e-commerce technology provider enables grocery stores to allow people to order through their mobile devices and have the groceries delivered. The application is tied in to the inventory management system and rewards program for consumers. E-commerce and payment players such as Enterworks and Payveris are also tied in to the product information system and the payment process—all parts of a system designed to lower costs. This creates a more efficient workflow where everything is optimized, waste is reduced, and the savings are shared with the consumer.

As a result, not only can the parent pick up fifty-five minutes of quality time with her child, she contributes to more efficiency, lower prices, and less food waste.

Great Ideas Give Way to New Ones
What lasts? Not much.

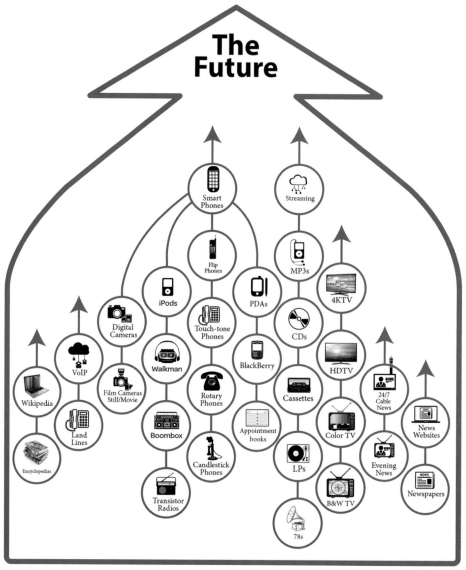

Ironically, the same dislocation happens to digital technology itself, as agile consumers flock to new innovations. Ask a young person if they use Facebook today, and the answer is likely to be "not that much. . . . I use Instagram and Snapchat instead." And they'll continue to do so, until the next thing comes along. That creates intense pressure to remain relevant and competitive.

Younger people tend to be more adaptable and quicker on the uptake. It's a familiar cliché: Parents routinely ask their kids to guide them through the latest tech; they struggle to wrap their minds around social platforms that teens immediately comprehend. Two-year-olds seem to be able to instinctively use a smartphone. I once saw a store display that featured a six-foot-high model of the latest Samsung smartphone. A toddler was standing in front of it, trying to make it work by slapping his hand on the screen. Adorable, and very telling.

Digital acceleration affects us all, and when it works its adoption seems so natural it's hard to remember the way things used to be. I was having a discussion with a coworker who was complaining about the lack of kiosks to check in to his flight at the airport. I remember in the early 2000s, when they first were launched in earnest, folks would refuse to approach a kiosk for something as important as their boarding pass for a flight. They wanted to interact with the person who issued the boarding pass directly. Today, many are not only annoyed that they have to go speak to an agent, but that they have to have a physical item at all. The next wave is the mobile boarding pass, which allows travelers to accomplish that mundane, lower-level function quicker and without the need for interaction with anything but their phone. Those who gain that time can then use it for more productive human interaction. Unfortunately, in the case of the hapless business traveler, it all too often means another conference call.

The World-Changing Power of Digital Engagement

Some aspects of our world are very slow to change, but once the door is opened, transformation comes rapidly. The political sphere was notoriously behind the times until the 2008 elections, when President Obama tapped into the relatively new power of social media to reach a whole new audience. Things haven't been the same since.

The 2016 U.S. presidential campaign was a fascinating look into how digital acceleration is continuing to change information consumption and, thereby, the media landscape. On one side we had Hillary Clinton, who ran a largely traditional campaign built around millions of dollars in television ad spending—paid media. On the other side we had Donald Trump, who made himself very available on social media and thrived on discussion of his controversial statements—earned media. Because he was such an irresistible news target, his name and his message were everywhere and he didn't have to pay to put it there.

These are examples of how traditional thinking about media no longer applies in a digital world. Media companies, steeped in business models that have stood the test of time, are struggling to adapt.

How does this technology-driven role-changing relate to media? For good or ill, digital acceleration is redefining our place in the media landscape. As we become more adaptable and accepting of change, traditional roles and limits become less relevant. Individuals are now involved in more of the process of storytelling; that makes their task more complex and time-consuming, but it's also positive in that they have more control over what happens. Filmmakers, television producers, photographers, digital artists, coders, musicians, and authors can take part in more of—or even all of—the process, making and distributing their own work with astonishingly good results.

More to the point, they're becoming more adept and comfortable with their expanding role. An indie filmmaker could easily be a writer, producer, director, film editor, and even special-effects artist all rolled into one. The singer-songwriter is becoming a singer-songwriter-producer–recording engineer–marketer-distributor-business manager. This is happening now; the world just needs to catch up.

OVER TIME, THINGS GET SIMPLER—BUT DOES THAT HELP?

As technology evolves, the way we interact with it tends to become less complex. This has always been true: When automobiles were introduced, they were complicated, finicky, and required constant adjustment and repair. Early race car drivers carried mechanics with them. Any of us who took auto shop in high school and could proudly complete routine maintenance on our vehicle know the feeling of buying a car today and never looking under the hood. We've learned that we wouldn't know what to do anyway, with most repairs and diagnostics done automatically by the vehicle through software-enabled monitoring tools. Now, cars have become ubiquitous, incredibly reliable transportation appliances, and we're rapidly approaching a future in which electric cars that drive themselves will change the experience and utility of a vehicle. That has the potential to change lives by making the commute a productive time to interact with others (in the vehicle or online), read, relax, or rest. On the other hand, the romance and freedom of the open road may become a distant memory—like those stories of walking to the store with your grandparents to buy groceries.

Likewise, the first home computers needed to be programmed by the user, and even commercially successful machines like the original IBM PC required complex commands to function. No longer. We've now reached the point at which technology is starting to become invisible. We don't think of computers as "computers" anymore. They're now masquerading as watches, telephones, thermostats, refrigerators—all the trappings of everyday life. My toothbrush has a microchip in it that tells it when to shut off, and my bathroom scale automatically uploads my weight to the health-tracking app on my phone. We interact with all of this technology in very ordinary ways without a second thought.

The same thing tends to happen with processes. Over time, it becomes easier to get things done. In part, this is due to acclimatization; today, any schoolkid knows what fonts and point sizes are. Before word processors, that knowledge was largely the domain of professional designers and typesetters. The same goes for the knowledge that allows us to use technology; once-obscure concepts like URLs, e-mail addresses, and the cloud are second nature these days.

This comfort with technology doesn't stem entirely from familiarity. Those who create the products, processes, and services that allow people to be productive are constantly looking to make things simpler, more streamlined, and better integrated. The media industry is not there yet, to be sure; creating and distributing a video game, film, or album is still an unnecessarily complex set of processes requiring a great deal of technical knowledge.

So, while on a small scale things get easier over time, zoom out and they're still quite complex. That's a social and organizational issue that directly impacts the roles we play. A siloed, disconnected process that's simpler than it used to be will still be siloed and disconnected. Technology tools that in themselves are easy to use but which don't work well together still pose a barrier to productivity. Those disconnects are at the heart of some of the biggest problems faced by the media industry, because they increase overall cost and complexity.

UNLOCKING OUR TRUE POTENTIAL

Digitization has allowed humans to connect more powerfully, intimately, and efficiently than ever before. Like so many areas of our lives that are becoming digital, so too are the stories we tell. We can now digitize any media asset—converting it to a series of ones and zeros—and in so doing, open up a whole new world of possibilities.

Think about the implications of digitization on the most fundamental level. The essence of the story is in how those ones and zeroes are connected to one another. If a story is fully digitized, everything from how it was imagined to how it's delivered can be changed with relative ease. Because there is no physical "thing" associated with data, the story can, in theory, be altered at will—changing its form and meaning—by rearranging the data, duplicating it, or converting it to another format. In the hands of a skilled craftsman, storyteller, or distributor, digitization changes everything.

All forms of media, from the written word to sounds, images, video, or a combination of any of them, can now be enhanced in countless ways, opening up whole new worlds for storytellers to explore. Immersive technologies are emerging that allow storytellers to engage the consumer in much more intimate, powerful, and creative ways. We even have interfaces that can directly convert thoughts and expressions into digital instructions that operate devices designed to enrich the lives of quadriplegics and other physically challenged individuals.

Because we can digitize virtually anything imaginable, we're on the cusp of making digital connections that will allow us to communicate in ways we can scarcely imagine, and the shift is likely to happen rapidly. Look back just a few years and consider how far we've come, and how fast. PDAs like the Palm Pilot and BlackBerry were life-changing for professionals. Now, billions have powerful computers connected to the whole world, and lives are being changed in an even more dramatic way. We're moving from mobile devices to wearables to the possibility of direct neural interfaces. What seemed like science fiction not long ago is now upon us, and as frightening as a neural connection to a digital ecosystem might sound, try the Oculus Rift virtual reality experience and assess for yourself what you think the natural next step is likely to be.

As we embrace new technology and weave it into our lives, new ways of participating in the media landscape will emerge and old roles will continue to evolve.

This opens up exciting possibilities. We are now seeing, for the first time, a general acceptance of how technology can improve almost every aspect of how we live. Now more than ever, individuals can see the power of bringing people together, automating lower-level functions, and unleashing the true creative power of a collective community. It's becoming less about the details of the process and more about the outcome.

The key is in finding a way to coordinate all that activity, eliminating the barriers between individuals, organizations, and workflows that currently exist across the media landscape. Once those lower-level functions are automated and aligned, they can become effectively invisible, even taken for granted. The flow from creation to production, monetization, and final consumption can accelerate. That allows us to focus on the power of human connections and allows us to return to what matters most: the enduring need to share our stories and experiences with one another . . . the joy of storytelling.

A Storyteller's Perspective: Digitization Has Revolutionized Music Creation

The general listening public became aware of the digitization of music in 1982, with the advent of the Compact Disc. But as early as the late 1970s, musicians had already begun to discover the exciting possibilities of digital sampling as a means of re-creating the richness of acoustic instrument sounds via keyboard synthesizers, with instruments like the Fairlight CMI (Computer Musical Instrument). Mapping acoustic sounds onto an electronic keyboard brought an incredible palette of sonic possibilities to musicians.

In 1983, the Musical Instrument Digital Interface (MIDI) furthered the revolution in how musicians performed with synthesizers and samplers, giving them the ability to capture, store, and edit performances via MIDI-sequencing technology—literally recording the notes, rather than the sounds, being played by a musician as a sequence of digital events in time. This allowed us to capture a performance in a computer, then change the speed of the playback without changing the pitch and edit the individual note by pitch, timing, and duration. It even allows us to re-orchestrate music by changing the instrumental sound on playback. With a musical performance stored as MIDI data on the computer, tools such as Avid's Sibelius allow a performance to also be displayed and edited in standard musical notation.

In 1991, Digidesign (now Avid) revolutionized the recording and production process by bringing the power of multitrack digital recording to personal computers with the release of Pro Tools hardware and software. Combining digital audio with the power of MIDI sequencing gave birth to the Digital Audio Workstation (DAW), changing the landscape for creative musicians to compose, orchestrate, perform, and record music in the digital domain. And with the birth of the World Wide Web in 1994, digital musicians had a new way to distribute and promote their music directly to their fans anywhere on the globe.

Just a few decades ago, composers heard music in their creative minds, but to hear that music as sound, they would have to first translate what they were imagining into symbols (musical notation), write them by hand using pencil and paper, and then give those symbols to other musicians as instructions to perform, thus creating the sound for the composer. Often the time between musical conception and realization was days or weeks, and sometimes it was never even possible. Today, composers can hear the music they are composing in real time and change any aspect of that music as they listen, interacting with sound as they work, just as a sculptor or painter works in their medium of expression.

—David Mash, senior vice president for innovation, strategy, and technology at Berklee College of Music

I imagine the Industrial Revolution must have felt the same way. It was a time when it was not only assumed that there was a better way to process a good or service; there was an openness and excitement for what the future might hold, and as a result, a fantastic environment for new ideas to come forward.

By enabling roles to change, technology can give us more time for creative pursuits. Game designers can focus on the experiences they create instead of the code they write. Journalists can devote their scarce time and resources to pursuing stories that will make a difference to people, instead of the complexities of communication, production, and distribution. Musicians can spend more time making music. Writers, actors, and artists of all kinds can spend more time practicing their crafts. Filmmakers can spend more time creating their next masterpiece (and tracking down financial backers). Whatever we do, the efficiency and empowerment that springs from technology gives all of us more choices in life, which allows us to share more of ourselves with people who have common interests. Everyone benefits.

PART 2

How Did We Get Here?

CHAPTER 4

We Are Technological Beings

We keep moving forward, opening new doors, and doing new things, because we're curious and curiosity keeps leading us down new paths.

—Walt Disney

The title of this chapter might raise a few eyebrows. Surely, we as humans are not defined solely by the tools we create. That's true. But consider this: Technology has always been part of our evolution, a constant companion that has fundamentally shaped the way we express ourselves—and in turn, altering us both on a societal and individual level.

Today, we equate technology with the electronic and mechanical devices that have become an integral part of our lives. But that's not what the word actually means. Its root—the Greek *techni*—means art and skill. The end of the word—*ology*—is the study or lore of something.

Knowing this, the very idea of technology becomes more closely associated with creativity than with the tools we use. Even the most fundamental forms of human expression—speech and movement—are intimately tied to technology when viewed through this lens. There is *technique* (there's that *techni* root again) to singing and dancing, neither of which require any tools at all. In a very real sense we've been using technology ever since we began telling stories to one another, and long before we started creating complex tools or the devices that we now label as "technology."

Storyteller's Perspective: Technology Empowers Us All

When we talk about technology, it doesn't necessarily pertain to computers; it pertains to the enhancement of human application. Technology is not just a program or an instrument; it's all the things that come together in sync to support human expression. For example, look at a paintbrush—take the wood and bristles, put it together and dip it in paint, and then you have a tool that is a form of technology because it's an application. All things that exist are due to human application and our advancements in technology.

If you go back in time when we didn't have the Internet, televisions, radios, or even the written word, people only received information from those around them. Compare that to the constant and accessible flow of information we now have thanks to technology.

When it comes to music, technology has provided more time for the artist to be creative and less time spent being technical. Technology has removed all the technicalities you'd have to apply just by being a human, such as processing speed and memory recall. When I say technology supports music, it's like having an ocean and a yacht in front of you. An ocean stands strong like music, and technology is the boat used to travel across it. As it pertains to music and digitizing joy, without technology, the traveling of information would not be as rapid, fluid, and successful. Without technology, the artists wouldn't be able to create the music that provides consumers with so much joy on a consistent basis.

Whatever technology is used to help support recording music also supports joy for people who can hear that music. And isn't that the goal?

—Jesse Wilson, music producer for Snoop Dogg, Justin Bieber, Ne-Yo, Celine Dion, *Birth of a Nation*, *Empire*, and many more

ALTERING PERCEPTION: THE CGI REVOLUTION

There is an inseparable link between technology and creativity. The tools we *use* to create affect *what* we create. That's as true of artistic expression as of any field of human endeavor, and perhaps nowhere is its impact more keenly felt than in visual media.

Those old enough to remember how radically different the original *Star Wars* was from what had come before can attest to this link between the technology of storytelling and the impact of the story itself. George Lucas and John Dykstra rewrote the book on special effects with computer-controlled motion photography and masterful blending of practical (i.e., physical) effects, animatronics, and pioneering digital effects. Essentially, Lucas and his team invented from scratch the digital tools that brought the *Star Wars* universe to life. Remember that *Star Wars* was created in the mid-1970s, when high school students were still using slide rules; even pocket calculators were still relatively new at the time.

Later, building on the techniques pioneered with the original film, Lucas founded Industrial Light & Magic and pushed the envelope by creating fully rendered characters and environments that were entirely digitized. Without that work, filmmaking as we now know it would not be possible.

Besides revolutionizing many aspects of visual-effects techniques, George Lucas also helped to pioneer digital editing technologies. In the mid-1980s, long before the advent of the Avid Media Composer, Lucasfilm incubated a technology division called Droid Works and Convergence Corporation, which developed the EditDroid, one of the first digital editing systems. EditDroid used a combination of LaserDisc players, custom software running on a Sun-1 computer, and a specialized hardware controller designed to emulate a traditional film editing "KEM" interface. Although the EditDroid was never a commercial success, it demonstrated the creative advantages of nonlinear editing and helped pave the way for the tools we use today. It was the beginning of the digitization of the entire workflow.

A Storyteller's Perspective: The Effect of VFX on Storytelling

When I started working in film editing, visual effects played a very small role in most films. Today, I get scripts where entire characters or scenes are full CGI and can be reimagined at any time during the post process. This means that the scriptwriting process is still going on during post. It's not that this hasn't been the case for a long time—editing is the final rewrite of any film. But the options have expanded; now we can manipulate the picture as well as add additional dialogue.

It's a complicated process. For instance, on Star Trek: Into Darkness, *Kirk and Kahn are jumping from the* Enterprise *to the enemy ship, through space, targeting a tiny open door on the enemy ship. What's the shortest, easiest way to explain how they do it to an audience? We had effects put a visual guidance system in their helmets so that the audience could track their progress without having to rely on voice-over. Pretty cool.*

In Star Wars: The Force Awakens, *we got to play with the character of Maz Kanata until we hit on just the right attitude and emotion needed for her scenes. There are upsides and downsides to this freedom. One can come up with so many ideas, but exploring those ideas is pricey and takes time to see through to completion.*

There are many films in which visual effects do drive the story—not on an emotional level but certainly on a practical one. You take a film like Ex Machina—*they created a way to keep the actor present in a realistic robot body. You believe that Alicia Vikander is that robot, and she retains her humanity. The film's emotional core depends on her character evoking emotion. It's this subtle, beautiful combination of actor and visual effects that makes the film successful both visually and emotionally.*

> *It's a challenge to stay on point, not get carried away and let the "tail wag the dog." I believe that when you watch a movie, you're following the emotion. The acting and the story are driving that, and if things aren't clicking emotionally, it doesn't matter how great the visual effects are—one can become disengaged if those other elements aren't in place. The most successful films for me are the ones in which the VFX and photography meld into one and I feel like it was all filmed. It feels real.*
>
> —Maryann Brandon, editor, A.C.E.
> (*Star Wars: Episode VII—The Force Awakens*)

The computer-generated imagery (CGI) that Lucas helped to pioneer has made it possible to create new worlds of breathtaking detail and realism, like the planet Pandora in James Cameron's *Avatar*. The technology has advanced to the point where its use is so routine and transparent that it stays out of the way of storytelling. Just as with computing devices and broadband connectivity, we've gotten so used to it that it's become invisible, accepted, and even expected.

Back in the days of big-screen Technicolor epics like 1963's *Cleopatra*, creating those worlds was an effort so massive and costly that it was rarely attempted. That one film, the most expensive in history up to that time, nearly bankrupted 20th Century Fox. It reportedly racked up cost overruns of 2,000 percent, and the final cost exceeded $42 million in 1963 dollars—approaching $330 million in today's money.[1,2]

Now, the technology exists to convincingly take us anywhere in space and time, and all it takes is imagination, an artist's eye, computer skills, software, and processing power. The same is true for immersive video games. Computers are even transforming the way broadcasters pursue their craft, enabling them to use augmented and virtual reality to enhance the story. Digital tools are having the effect of removing limits on what is possible.

The utterly convincing virtual worlds that are now commonplace stand in stark contrast to what could be achieved before powerful computing and automation became so widely available. The technological limits that existed before CGI and motion capture shaped storytelling just as much as the latest digital effects do. Most special effects in the 1960s and 1970s were ridiculously primitive by today's standards. One close look at "Bruce," the mechanical shark in *Jaws*, would make an audience laugh, even in the (by today's standards) unsophisticated world of 1975. But *Jaws* was incredibly frightening because, without a convincing shark to look at, the movie had to be about the unseen but ever-present menace.

Taking effects to a new level is one of the things that made *Star Wars* so amazing at the time. Even though the effects relied on computer-controlled cameras rather than CGI, that technological advancement marked a breakthrough in visual storytelling.

Audiences are now far more sophisticated and demanding. We expect perfection, and we get it. In 2015's Academy Award–winning *Mad Max: Fury Road*, Charlize Theron's character is an amputee. The effect is utterly convincing and is incorporated seamlessly into her performance. It's a story element made possible through technology—once again, the tools shape the way the story is told by adding dimension to a key character.

Media companies are also going back to earlier work to improve the way stories are told, using better technology to remaster old properties and, in some cases, alter what came before. Watch an episode of the original *Star Trek* series today, and you'll find that all the effects shots have been replaced with CGI. To purists and those old enough to remember the original prints, it's a bit upsetting—but for today's audiences, it makes the show better.

Technology also opens up new forms of expression that were never before possible. The invention of the piano, for example, radically changed orchestral music and led to some of the most beautiful compositions ever heard—pieces impossible to conceive without that technology. And one of the very first motion pictures, 1902's *Le Voyage Dans La Lune*, was a science-fiction film that used previously unimagined special effects to tell the story. To be sure, not every innovation catches on. The eerie wail of the Theremin electronic musical instrument—so familiar from classics like *The Day the Earth Stood Still*—became a staple of B-movie science fiction in the 1950s, but it's not exactly commonplace these days.

What's Real?

There's an interesting aspect to the high degree of realism found in today's digital effects: with perfection so commonplace, people no longer have any reliable way of telling whether what they see and hear is real or fiction. When extended beyond entertainment into areas such as politics, propaganda, and news, the possibilities and impact of manipulating reality are frightening. This can be readily seen in the widespread and increasing belief in conspiracy theories—and the efforts to debunk them. But at the same time, this phenomenon has led to growing skepticism about the validity of imagery and increased scrutiny of information sources. Trusting the evidence of your own eyes is no longer something you can count on.

Like all technologies, hyper-realistic special effects and other reality-bending advancements like virtual and augmented reality are not inherently good or bad. Like all tools, the use to which they are put is guided by society. They can be used for manipulation, coercion, or deception—or to enhance, accentuate, and enrich the story and give a clearer view of the truth. As the tools become more powerful, age-old questions of how to best use them take on new importance and place a greater burden of responsibility on storytellers. Ultimately, the employment of such tools is governed by society through laws, practices, and social norms. What we create is no more or less than a reflection of who we are.

ENHANCING REALITY TO TELL MORE COMPELLING STORIES

Advanced tools for virtual and augmented reality are driving the latest trends in digital media. On-air graphics are widely used in news coverage to add depth and counterpoint to the story, helping influence opinion and engage viewers. This kind of digital enhancement is also becoming commonplace in sports, where digital overlays "paint" markers on a football field and show the trajectory of the ball. A play can now be frozen and digitally "explored" from multiple angles, frame by frame. The result is a far more interesting, engaging story.

M6, a European media company, recently won an award for its use of advanced augmented reality and graphics technology. It showed what appeared to be an in-person discussion on the sidelines of a soccer match, between the studio host and a person in the stadium. Of course, the host never left the green-screen studio, and the whole sequence was carefully scripted. At one point the host even carried an umbrella to match those being held pitch-side to enhance the illusion. In another example, a player at the event appeared on the studio set to be interviewed, even though he was many miles away.

The *Pokémon Go* Phenomenon

In the summer of 2016, almost literally overnight a new augmented reality game seized the public's imagination. *Pokémon Go* was something new because it made the real world part of game play, the very definition of augmented reality. Players had to visit real locations to play the game.

The experience was so compelling that the growth was almost unbelievable. Within two days of its release, 3 percent of all Android users in the United States were playing the game daily, a usage rate comparable to Twitter. In two days! And they were spending more time playing than using social media platforms such as WhatsApp, Snapchat, and Instagram.[3]

The craze made international news and led to some interesting—and bizarre—outcomes. Local businesses were using it to drive traffic and reaping huge boosts in sales. Criminals were using it to lure victims. Teens in the U.K. lost their way chasing Pokémon, got trapped in a cave, and had to be rescued.[4] Players were getting so distracted that two men actually fell from a cliff while playing.[5]

While ultimately a passing fad, the *Pokémon Go* phenomenon graphically shows the power of digital storytelling—and the immediacy of digital media.

Adding digital elements to live video is just the beginning. Where cinematographers have traditionally controlled what the audience could see by carefully framing every shot, today's virtual and augmented reality technologies are revolutionizing the viewing experience and offering new ways to create immersive storytelling experiences. By simplifying the creation of virtual environments, real or imagined, they help unlock the storyteller's imagination without the massive investment in time and money that was once required.

With VR, rather than looking through a window onto a scene, audience members are immersed into the scene and have the freedom to look around and follow wherever their attention takes them. And with today's augmented reality tools, storytellers are blending together traditional "live action" content with computer-generated content—all in real time. Using green screens and today's AR technology, a commentator can be visually transported from a studio directly onto the sidelines of a sporting event and back again. After the game, a player can seem to be teleported from the arena onto a chair in a studio thousands of miles away for an interview. In this way, the latest storytelling technologies are, in a sense, cheating the time-space continuum.

OUR LIVES—AND OURSELVES—HAVE BEEN SHAPED BY TECHNOLOGY

Technology, of course, is about much more than the means we use to communicate and express ourselves. As humans, we have always turned to technological developments to make our lives better in every way. The very evolution of our species has been shaped by technology.

The technology of cooking allowed our distant ancestors to gain more nourishment from our food, which spurred the development of our brains. The wheel simplified transportation, transforming society by allowing us to gather in cities and have food brought to us, and interact with other humans from far away. Ropes, pulleys, and levers meant we could move heavier objects with less muscle power, changing our bodies. Metalworking allowed us to make superior tools and weapons, improving our living standard and making us more secure. Writing allowed us to preserve what we learned for future generations and share it with our contemporaries. The list goes on and on. The link between technology and our advancement runs throughout history; the story of humanity is very much the story of the technologies we've created.

The digital networks that connect us and dominate today's world are no different. Computational innovation and connectivity have become embedded in our existence in ways we could never have imagined. It's not a stretch to say that civilization as we know it depends on digital technology.

Without computers and broadband, the global economy would collapse almost overnight. That wouldn't be the end of the world, of course—after all, we did quite well for a very long time without digital technology—but just try to imagine how your life would change without it. Would you have a job to go to? Would you be able to access money or buy anything? Would society function in a recognizable way? Perhaps more importantly on a personal level, would you actually suffer withdrawal symptoms? I think it's quite likely you would. Technology has—*is*—rewiring our brains.

As technology becomes more powerful and simpler, and the connectivity infrastructure becomes more robust, our entire lives are being reengineered. Now we are always connected, able to access information, entertainment, and other people anywhere we go. And the distinction between the tools we use for work and for personal life management are evaporating. We now expect everything we do in life to be simpler, more ubiquitous, and intuitive. Everything should just *work* without us having to think about which platform, software, process, service, or file format to use. The technology we rely upon should be, and increasingly is, transparent to us.

CHAPTER 5

The Effect of Technology on Behavior

Where do we go? Oh, where do we go now?

—Guns N' Roses

The technology we choose to incorporate into our lives fundamentally impacts our expectations and perceptions of the world. That, in turn, influences our behavior. This isn't a recent development. Before the invention of the clock, the very idea of keeping a schedule was nonsensical; the day began at sunrise and ended at sunset, and that was that. But with the ability to readily tell time, whole new patterns of behavior emerged—patterns that have become so familiar that we no longer give them any thought. With regular schedules, it became possible to collaborate more easily and work toward a common goal, setting the stage for the way we work today. The behavior sparked by a technological innovation became deeply ingrained into social norms.

This interplay between technology and behavior is something we encounter every day. Your phone is one of the first things you look at in the morning and one of the last things you look at when you go to bed. It vibrates and, without thinking, you reach for it to check the text you received because that's how you've been conditioned to respond. Technology is changing how we function as social creatures and even how we think. We routinely engage in social interactions that are part face-to-face and part immersion in the digital realm, with people talking to one another while also interacting with their devices.

Even the language we use to express ourselves has been altered, seemingly overnight, by technology. *LOL* was added to the Oxford Dictionary in 2011; WTF happened to words, anyway? Memes have become convenient conduits for jokes and sarcasm in online communications. We're now seeing whole conversations happen using nothing but emoji.

Asking someone to join you for a drink after work isn't what it used to be.

This embedding of technology into our lives even impacts the way people experience their surroundings. I once saw a person in the crowd at the New York Marathon filming the event with an iPad. His entire interaction with the world was through that screen. I had to wonder if he really had any sense of actually being there, or if the act of recording it was necessary to make the experience "real" for him. His immersion in digital reality, even as he was present in the physical space, was not unlike what we saw with *Pokémon Go*.

The line between real experience and the virtual world is blurring rapidly. Runners can now participate in marathons, and cyclists can take group bike rides, in a virtual space. Using connected exercise equipment, they can share the experience with others who are doing the same, seeing the course and the location of other athletes without ever leaving the room.

Virtual reality is also putting people where they could never actually be with surprising fidelity. In 2016, the Isle of Man TT (a high-speed motorcycle race in the U.K.) put 360-degree video technology on some of the bikes, allowing people to don a VR headset and see what it's actually like to ride a motorcycle at 150 mph with the freedom to look around in any direction. At the 2016 Summer Olympics in Rio, NBC captured more than 100 hours of virtual-reality video for everything from the opening and closing ceremonies to gymnastics, diving, and fencing, providing an unprecedented immersive viewing experience. As thrilling as all of this can be, of course, it's still an experience limited to video and audio—for now.

Technology is also making it possible to enrich and add new dimensions to the live experience. This is happening now at sporting events, where live stats, video feeds, and social media feeds are made available via handheld devices and apps. Combined with augmented reality, the total experience becomes very compelling indeed.

All of this is creating a new, hybrid experience that combines the real with the digital—a new form of storytelling that is richer than any of the individual experiences that go into it.

These enhanced experiences can have a profound impact on behavior, because they alter what we look for and what we respond to. If we know, for example, that instant replay in a stadium will show us exactly what happened on the field a moment ago in great detail, we're less likely to pay close attention to the live action. If we're at a concert, we're more likely to watch the giant video screen behind the stage than the faraway performer. We could get those digital experiences at home, of course . . . but we wouldn't *be* there.

For some categories of live events, such as concerts, demand remains high, while in other categories attendance is waning. One wonders if in the future attendance at live events will plummet as the digital experience begins to outstrip the real one. It's already true that the television view of a sporting event or performance allows people in the audience to see far more than they could in person, but it lacks the feeling of being present. Once that difference starts to erode, the social experience of a mass gathering might begin to lose its meaning and impact.

Much of this behavioral shift has come about only in the past few years, driven by the Internet and broadband. Continuous connectivity anytime, anywhere is now seen as normal.

Pervasive connectivity is changing basic attitudes and points of view. Why even attempt to remember anything when information can be so easily found online? Why bother to own music and movies, or rely on broadcast media, when content can be so easily streamed? Why buy a paper book when a whole library can be loaded onto a Kindle? Even more significantly, why engage in a difficult debate when we can dive into the digital echo chamber and choose to listen only to those with whom we agree? Critical-thinking skills and well-worn patterns of behavior and thought, developed over centuries, are evaporating like morning dew in the face of continuous immersion in the digital realm.

When Media and Reality Collide

Technology sometimes influences our perceptions in odd ways. Orson Welles's famous 1938 *War of the Worlds* broadcast is a classic case study of how perception and reality interact.

Even though the broadcast was clearly identified as a radio drama at the beginning, many listeners tuned in just late enough to be fooled by a seemingly live orchestral broadcast that rapidly became what appeared to be a genuine reporter-in-the-field account of an actual event.

The uproar that ensued, as some people came to believe that Martians had in fact landed, is the stuff of legend.

What's interesting about this event is that by 1938 people had come to unquestioningly accept what they heard on the radio as fact, provided it bore the trappings of a real news broadcast. It should be noted that the watershed live coverage of the *Hindenburg* disaster ("Oh, the humanity!") had taken place only a year before.

This willing acceptance of content as long as it's packaged in a believable form and meets our expectations is still happening and, if anything, is getting worse. All it takes is a quick perusal of Facebook to find many examples of rumors and outright untruths circulated as fact, even when they've been conclusively disproven.

While as a society we've become more aware of the role that media plays in our view of the world, just as with the tools used to create it, media is neither good nor bad in itself. Ultimately storytelling is a reflection of human nature, shaped by our social conscience, and nothing more. The real question is one of consequences—is the intent to mislead or shape the "truth" as the storyteller sees it? Is the outcome what was sought? In the case of the *War of the Worlds* broadcast, the fallout was clearly unexpected.

WE CHANGE WHAT WE SEE AND HEAR, AND IT CHANGES US

The unending flood of information that continuous connectivity provides has eroded the influence of media, especially when it comes to journalism. With no filter and no single trusted version of the "truth," it's harder to know what to believe and harder still to hold groups accountable. Instant access, the rise of citizen journalism, and the 24/7 news cycle have changed the way we consume media.

Media companies are willing participants in this dilution, working flat-out to customize what they provide to fit the consumers' tastes. People used to have to spend a lot of time on lower-level functions to get to the story—buying and reading the paper, devoting time to the evening news, and perhaps reading more in-depth reporting in a weekly news magazine. But as the tools have advanced and the number of choices have increased, less commitment is necessary; we don't have to seek out the news because it comes to us, and increasingly it's rebalanced and skewed to suit our preferences.

That's led to intense competition for the consumer's precious time. We need not waste time on content that does not interest us or that we disagree with, because we can readily find someone who will tell us exactly what we want to hear. For news outlets, understanding the news that is important to communities has become increasingly complicated, as is coping with the growth in choice among consumption channels. Not only do news providers have to focus on the relevant stories, they must also find ways to make those stories available in a way that fits the consumer's lifestyle, all as the stories themselves unfold.

A Storyteller's Perspective: The Evolution of the Newsroom and Technology

Using today's technology to produce the news is truly a wonderful experience. We can shoot high definition video, edit it on a laptop in the field and send it back to the newsroom instantly via the Internet. We can blog, tweet, Instagram and post to our websites, and still have time to cover extra news stories. Using our cell phones, we can send live video back to the station or to any other point in our network.

A lot has changed since I started in this business. Newsroom computer systems didn't exist. Journalists used typewriters to write their stories, and producers did the rundown and tracked the day's events on a chalkboard. The Rolodex was a reporter's most valued possession. Typewriters with large type were used to produce the show's scripts on lengths of paper to be used in the teleprompter, which consisted of a black and white camera shooting down on the paper as it was pulled across the teleprompter deck and projected onto a monitor behind the two-way glass in front of the lens on the TV camera.

16mm film cameras were used to capture news in the field. For a big story, you would rush the film back to the station and wait until it was developed. Only then could you view it on a film viewer (a mini projector) and edit the story on a film splicer. The reporter would write the story, in some cases, without ever having seen the finished film piece. Because you couldn't view your film until it was developed, you didn't know if you truly captured that "Oh my God" moment—the image that could make a small story big.

The breakthrough came with three quarter-inch videotape and the shoulder-mounted camera. If you had a portable monitor, you could look at what you shot in the field. This technology increased efficiency for news gatherers and, in my opinion, the quality and quantity of what we could cover as a news organization.

Today, using file-based workflows and Internet connectivity, we can move the complete storytelling process even closer to source. A multimedia journalist with a laptop and a camera can spend the entire day newsgathering and may not have to come back to the TV station at all. Their productivity goes up, and so can the quality of their stories.

This technology, along with digital distribution outlets, has transformed newsrooms into content centers that publish news 24 hours a day. Our presence on second screen and mobile devices frees us from the constraints of a fixed time slot for the evening news. As long as someone has access to a screen of any kind, they can be plugged into our news cycle 24/7.

Technological advances may have changed the process of storytelling, but there usually still is a trusted anchor person delivering the news in front of the camera. When Walter Cronkite, Edward R. Murrow, Tom Brokaw, and Barbara Walters came into our living rooms every night to deliver the news, they were among the most trusted people in America. Journalists employed by traditional news outlets operate within an editorial process that vets their stories and sources, and that is generally "trusted."

In contrast, today, anyone with a cell phone and a social media account can be a journalist. Since many people get their news from the Internet, we should be concerned about losing the paradigm of a "trusted source." News may or may not have undergone the same careful editorial process we have come to expect, and, in fact, may originate from sources that could be questionable. Since hacking has become rampant, how do we know that the stories we read, are, in fact, real?

As technology allows news content to be produced and distributed by diverse sources, how does our audience determine who is a trusted source? Even worse, what if the audience doesn't care if the source is trusted and the story is being truthfully reported? Freedom of speech and freedom of the press are a valued privilege enshrined in our Constitution. As a news organization, we have an obligation to tell the truth. Regardless of the technology used to report and disseminate it, we must always continue to tell the truth in order to remain a "trusted source."

—Delbert R. Parks III, senior vice president and chief technology officer,
Sinclair Broadcast Group

Diversity of opinion is the first casualty of today's competitive, customization-driven environment; objective truth is the second. It's easy to find unsupported opinion masquerading as independent, objective journalism, and such content is readily accepted as fact. This has led to an extreme polarization of society, and that has had a corrosive effect on trust in our institutions.

Interest groups have gotten much more sophisticated in how they use this new media landscape to shape opinion. But we as consumers are also all too ready to swallow the message. At times the distortion of reality can reach absurd proportions, as demonstrable facts and outright lies are simply ignored. This is particularly true in the political arena.

This is not an indictment of technology's impact on expression and communication—far from it. To be sure, in one sense it shows how willing we are to walk away from independent thought and the accumulation of knowledge. But on the flip side, we have the power to choose and judge for ourselves, provided we exercise it. No one is forcing us down the proverbial rabbit hole.

If I Say It, It Must Be True

The ability to shape public opinion and influence individuals has reached new heights, thanks to the proliferation of media outlets and the ability to bypass established gatekeepers. Extremist groups like ISIS use social media and YouTube as highly effective recruiting tools, bypassing traditional information sources to directly target their audience.

Even what we now think of as "mainstream" media is often highly biased, because of the drive to tailor and customize content to match audience preferences. This is how the "echo chamber" effect happens, and it provides a ready-made platform for those with an agenda to get their message out.

Measurement tools and analytics have become so sophisticated that it's possible to spin the message and its presentation in exactly the right way, and with incredible speed, to get an audience to respond positively. Doing so drives consumption and therefore revenue, so there's a powerful incentive to focus the narrative in a certain way.

Nevertheless, there's good reason to believe that attention spans are shrinking and we rely increasingly on others to tell us what to pay attention to. It's an issue of volume. Earlier we noted the dramatic increase in time spent consuming content—more than 50 percent[1]—but that pales in comparison to the far more dramatic rise in content creation, which has roughly quadrupled[2]

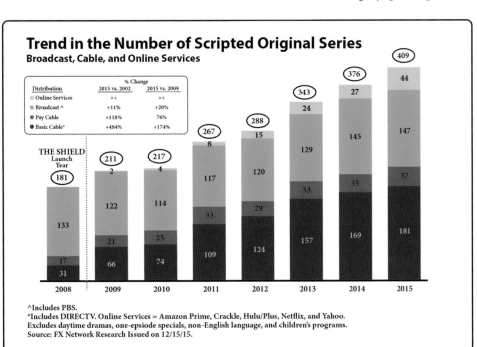

Content is exploding, far outstripping the ability of consumers to keep pace.

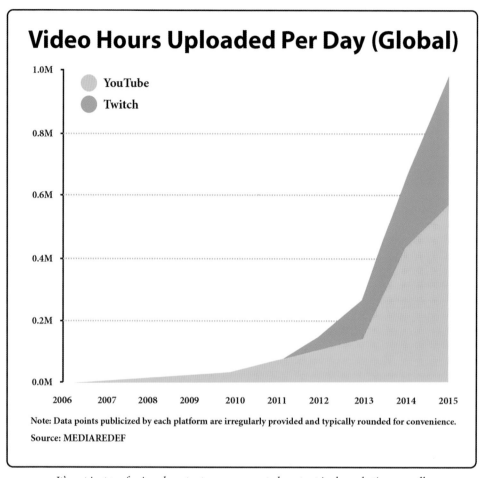

Video Hours Uploaded Per Day (Global)

YouTube

Twitch

Note: Data points publicized by each platform are irregularly provided and typically rounded for convenience.

Source: MEDIAREDEF

It's not just professional content; user-generated content is skyrocketing as well.

on a per-capita basis over the past decade. We have more choice than ever, and it's much more than we can possibly consume.

If there's a lesson to be learned, it's that more information is not automatically a good thing. There is now too much content for the time and attention we have to consume it, which by definition means a filter must be put in place. The question is, which filter?

Unable to sift our way through a vast sea of content, we naturally simplify the task and look to arbiters we trust, like ABC, CBS, NBC, or Fox News, maybe NPR, Oprah, Bloomberg, or CNBC, and crowd filters like lists of the top-ten songs and crowd-sourced movie reviews. We even shop and eat this way, choosing products by Amazon rankings and services by Yelp customer reviews rather than independent, objective research. In many areas of our lives, the opinions of others have become more important than our own.

The key is to have timely, relevant, and filtered content that helps us enhance our lives. That places an extra burden on us, as well as those we turn to, to embrace objectivity and commit to facts. The catch is that neither we nor the brands we trust have been able to figure out a way to truly break free from bias.

One important aspect of trust in media sources that must not be overlooked is the ability of a skilled editor with access to good tools and content to shape a story. Just because there's video footage, audio, or images of an event doesn't mean the depiction of that event is accurate. The truism that there are at least three versions of any story—yours, mine, and what really happened—applies to anything we might see or hear.

A Storyteller's Perspective: What Comes First, the Footage or the Story?

For many of the reality shows that I've edited, the process has consisted of producers shooting B-roll footage of a contestant on the show and an interview. Then we are asked to tell the person's life story in ninety seconds. The piece can be (and may be) cut in a number of different ways. The tone can be made somber and dramatic or funny and upbeat. There may be hours of footage to make a ninety-second segment, so the number of approaches to the story are nearly infinite.

In the end, the segment will be a version of what the producer had intended at the shoot, or the network will decide to tell an entirely different story using the same footage.

On most films, the story has been predetermined down to every line of dialogue, and most footage is shot for specific purposes to strengthen that story. Even though the arc of the story can change and certain things can be reshaped and reordered, many films follow the original intent of the script. On some occasions, I've been able to use my "unscripted brain" to help improve a movie, moving a key scene from the middle of the movie to the beginning, changing the overall tone of the film, or combining footage from two sides of two different phone conversations to create a new scene.

I always try to see all footage and dialogue in terms of the possibilities that may exist outside of the original intention, and remember that there's more than one way to approach footage of any kind.

—Jason Stewart, editor, The Amazing Race, The Voice, Extreme Makeover: Home Edition, World's Greatest Dad, Sleeping Dogs Lie

BLINDSIDED, IN A GOOD WAY: THE POSITIVE IMPACT OF TECHNOLOGY

While technology's effect on behavior can have a downside, there are overwhelming benefits. One of the most exciting things about the link between technology and behavior—especially creativity—arises from the amazing adaptability of humans. When we invent something, people have always used it in new and unexpected ways. Nowhere is this more apparent than the Internet. By enabling people everywhere to connect and embrace the fundamental need to share their experiences, it has led to a renaissance of knowledge sharing that no one could have foreseen. It is a reflection of who we are, at our best and at our worst.

But, at the same time, this endless choice has opened up the floodgates and made it much easier to access the wealth of human experience and interactions. Whether through broadband, Wi-Fi, or cellular networks, many of the changes we've seen in the modern era are a result of our worldwide connectivity, allowing an unprecedented advancement that includes accelerated learning and understanding of one another.

A Storyteller's Perspective: Humanity Must Be at the Core of the Digital Experience

The digital medium and practitioners of it often ignore a fundamental truism: Humanity will always be front and center and the most critical part of storytelling.

We're more connected now, yet we have less human interaction than ever. We should be more efficient but in reality are less so because of our digital communication. Texting is not faster than a phone call. Tweeting doesn't offer context.

Keeping humanity as a central tenet of a digital operating principle is the glue that binds us. Why? Because humanity in a digital world creates community. And community is something that the human condition craves, from Apple product fanboys to the Pokémon Go craze, from the success of Beats to the sharing economy of Uber, Twitter, or Instagram. Something in all those endeavors created a fervor, a demand, almost a movement.

This matters very much to those who make their living in the digital space. People pay for community if they feel a part of it. They will reward you with loyalty and scale, become evangelists, give valuable feedback. They won't do that just because they are connected. The ecosystem is full of companies that understand that—and even more companies that don't. The companies that aren't successful rarely have a technical issue; they have issues connecting to people. People who know how to insert and maintain humanity into the digital world are worth their weight in gold. It could be design, communication, the customer experience, interface, or any number of other elements that touch you. That human touch point separates you from the noise. It allows you to stand out.

My partner, Dave Pensado, and I have had success with our online television program Pensado's Place. *We are watched in 203 countries, and more than 150 schools use us as a teaching tool.*

Feedback to us is immediate. And we are responsive. Some of what we've heard over the past six years are words like "authentic," "original," "I feel like I know you," "trust," "friendly," "funny," "informative," "genuine," "emotional," "inspired," "aspirational," "I took your advice," "I can't believe you got in touch with me so quickly." These are not words driven by digital connection. They are words of humanity.

—Herb Trawick, executive producer and co-host, *Pensado's Place*

Today, thanks to technology, we can earn university degrees without ever meeting our professors or classmates face-to-face. We befriend people on the other side of the planet, exchange views as if they were our next-door neighbors, and think nothing of it. It's not remarkable, and that's what makes it so beautiful. The digital technology of communicating, of sharing, of storytelling, is part of who we are, and it's part of the shared human story.

Perhaps the clearest example of this creative energy is the impact of social media and its increasingly powerful influence on how we live. When the social media revolution of Web 2.0 came along, it was marked by a new idea that, when one thinks about it, is as old as storytelling itself. The technologies for sharing our experiences do not have to be designed with a particular purpose in mind. That's as simple as pen and paper, but in the world of electronic media, it was, for a long time, an alien idea. The people behind this new way of interacting realized that if they built the platform, people would figure out what it was good for. It wasn't necessary to rigidly define the technology's purpose.

The jury is still out on whether grand visions like this can sustain themselves in a reliable way; as of this writing Twitter has yet to make a profit,[3] yet the power of the idea behind it is so great that it continues to operate and grow. Meanwhile, other social media platforms, like Facebook, have been able to successfully turn the corner, while failed efforts, like MySpace, now seem like quaint experiments.

While the idea of an online interactivity service without specific purpose or theme was a difficult concept for many to grasp at the time, we've seen an amazing burst of creativity arising from giving people new ways to digitally share their stories. The Arab Spring was a complete surprise, and it would never have happened without social media. Neither would important social movements like Black Lives Matter.

A Storyteller's Perspective: Sharing the Storyteller's Journey

Criticism in the music industry is one of the hardest things to deal with as an artist. After my appearance on America's Got Talent, *I was expected to blow up. But I was lost in an industry with sharks who wanted to mold me into what they thought I should be. I never hid that I was gay, but it wasn't known to many folks, and I was afraid to be completely out. I was told to get a fake boyfriend, not to cut my hair, be more feminine, etc. Every song I wrote had to be a hit, and I couldn't freely express who I was, so I felt trapped.*

I eventually broke free of the people who were trying influence me and took a step back to reflect on why I wanted to pursue this career. I remembered why I chose to be an artist. I didn't want a 9-to-5 job; I knew I could creatively find a way to make money and wanted to influence the younger generation to follow their dreams.

I built my own website, created an account on every social media outlet possible, recorded all my ideas with my camera, and started to grow an online following. By posting videos and photos and telling my story, people felt like they were on my journey with me. I try to respond to everyone who comments because I am truly thankful for everyone who shares my content, and personal engagement is crucial to keep my business growing.

The harder I worked on myself and on my craft, the more confidence I gained and the less I let people's criticism get the best of me. It is, of course, important to be open to people wanting to help, but I have learned to sift through the bullshit and find the golden nuggets that remain. Most people want to help; they just don't know how to do it in a positive manner.

By accepting myself for who I am, and not letting criticism get the best of me. I now walk proudly and confidently through every door that has opened for me. I still have many more dreams I want to accomplish, but I know that I am on my way to an exciting, extraordinary career.

—Butterscotch, music artist, finalist on *America's Got Talent*

That same kind of inventive spirit—the urge to take available resources and create something new—is embedded in the human psyche. There are endless examples, from DJs coming up with scratching using turntables, to Les Paul effectively inventing multitrack recording using nothing but ingenuity and existing recording devices, to George Lucas pioneering digital editing with his groundbreaking work with the *Star Wars* franchise.

With each new advancement in technology and its use, the body of knowledge grows, and others take up the torch and run with it. They produce new variations, use the tools in yet more new ways, and add to the amazing diversity of storytelling in all its forms. Those with vision take ideas and are able to change the world because they see the potential, even if they don't clearly see where the idea might lead. A good example is the famous (and apocryphal) story of Steve Jobs having an epiphany when visiting Xerox PARC in 1979 and seeing a graphical user interface, which supposedly led to the Macintosh. As with many such stories, that isn't quite the way it happened. The GUI that PARC engineers had developed was already well known in the tech community, but they had no idea how to commercialize it. What Steve Jobs and Bill Gates brought to the table was an appreciation for its significance, and between them they launched the personal computer revolution.

When Technologies Converge, Wonderful Things Can Happen

Technology can be the driver of whole new forms of expression and storytelling. One need look no further than video games to see this taking place.

Put powerful computing, connectivity, and imagination together and amazing levels of creativity result. Today's game designers are true artists and storytellers, producing immersive experiences in stunningly beautiful and compelling worlds.

What makes this possible is not one realm of technology but several. Today's video games combine visual art, music, cinematic content, and interactivity in a unique fashion. In no other form of storytelling is it possible for the audience to become so deeply connected to the story itself.

Storytelling through video games and similar experiences is on the cusp of a golden age, as virtual-reality technology becomes more mainstream. *Pokémon Go* was just the beginning. Today's games may well spark a new kind of media—immersive films in which the audience can inhabit the scene alongside the characters, or virtual gathering places so real that they will provide a true alternative to physical interaction.

The process of ideas sparking new ideas and new creativity never ends, and it's accelerating. Driven by digitization, within our lifetimes the world has changed almost beyond recognition. Change is happening so fast that it's creating major disruption in long-standing institutions like journalism, film, broadcast media, and the music business. Everyone is struggling to get ahead of the curve, and where we're headed is far from clear.

CHAPTER 6

Technology and Work: Evolution in Parallel

Here's looking at you, kid.

—From *Casablanca*

When we consider the role that technology has played in shaping storytelling and the media industry as a whole, it's useful to step back and first look at how business processes progress over time, and the influence of technology on them. In most industries—and media is no exception—processes tend to be made scalable for growth, then automated and connected for efficiency. Technology plays an important role in this evolution.

The dual evolutionary paths of technology and its use in industry workflows have unfolded in parallel, with technological advancement making new ways of doing business possible, and changes in workflows in turn driving the next generation of technical innovation. It's an ever-rising spiral that puts increasing power and capability into the hands of the individual by making tasks simpler, but it's also the source of some fundamental issues that affect—and sometimes limit—the way we work.

Consider any application on your computer or phone. There will be things it does very well, things it might be able to accomplish after a fashion, and other things it's incapable of doing. How you work with, and think about, that application is limited by those capabilities. The tool itself influences our view of what can and cannot be done.

The key issue, and an important challenge facing businesses, is that while the evolution of technology and the evolution of how it is employed do take place in parallel, they do not progress at the same rate. It takes time for technology to deliver on its full potential, because there's a learning curve involved. People need to see the possibilities and build processes, organizations, and behaviors to capitalize on the new opportunity.

That can be disruptive to businesses and individuals alike, and there are winners and losers. Those who can adapt thrive, while those who can't keep up are at a severe disadvantage. Whole industries can be caught off guard and

Technological Advances Through the Years

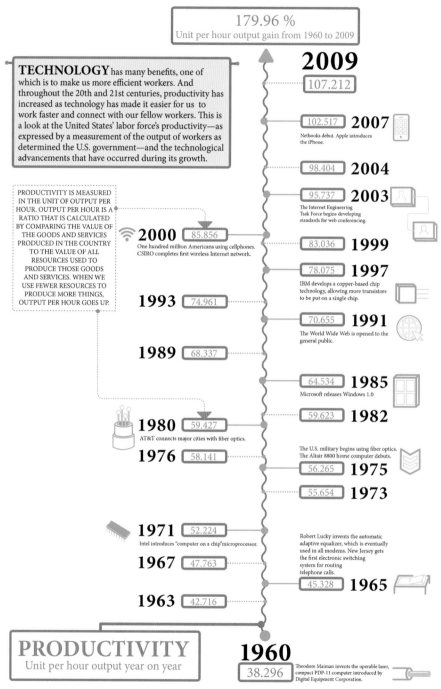

179.96 %
Unit per hour output gain from 1960 to 2009

TECHNOLOGY has many benefits, one of which is to make us more efficient workers. And throughout the 20th and 21st centuries, productivity has increased as technology has made it easier for us to work faster and connect with our fellow workers. This is a look at the United States' labor force's productivity—as expressed by a measurement of the output of workers as determined the U.S. government—and the technological advancements that have occurred during its growth.

PRODUCTIVITY IS MEASURED IN THE UNIT OF OUTPUT PER HOUR. OUTPUT PER HOUR IS A RATIO THAT IS CALCULATED BY COMPARING THE VALUE OF THE GOODS AND SERVICES PRODUCED IN THE COUNTRY TO THE VALUE OF ALL RESOURCES USED TO PRODUCE THOSE GOODS AND SERVICES. WHEN WE USE FEWER RESOURCES TO PRODUCE MORE THINGS, OUTPUT PER HOUR GOES UP.

2009
107.212

2007 102.517
Netbooks debut. Apple introduces the iPhone.

2004 98.404

2003 95.737
The Internet Engineering Task Force begins developing standards for web conferencing.

2000 85.856
One hundred million Americans using cellphones. CSIRO completes first wireless Internet network.

1999 83.036

1997 78.075
IBM develops a copper-based chip technology, allowing more transistors to be put on a single chip.

1993 74.961

1991 70.655
The World Wide Web is opened to the general public.

1989 68.337

1985 64.534
Microsoft releases Windows 1.0

1982 59.623

1980 59.427
AT&T connects major cities with fiber optics.

The U.S. military begins using fiber optics. The Altair 8800 home computer debuts.

1976 58.141

1975 56.265

1973 55.654

1971 52.224
Intel introduces "computer on a chip" microprocessor.

Robert Lucky invents the automatic adaptive equalizer, which is eventually used in all modems. New Jersey gets the first electronic switching system for routing telephone calls.

1967 47.763

1965 45.328

1963 42.716

PRODUCTIVITY
Unit per hour output year on year

1960
38.296

Theodore Maiman invents the operable laser, compact PDP-11 computer introduced by Digital Equipment Corporation.

As technological advances have been introduced, our productivity—both at the workplace and in our personal lives—has skyrocketed. The world is a far more complex and interconnected place than it once was because of technology, and it's only with technology that we're able to manage our journey through it.

find themselves struggling for survival. We're seeing that today in areas like the cable TV market; it's hard to justify spending $100 a month on cable when most content is available from streaming services for a fraction of the cost.

FROM SCALE TO EFFICIENCY: DEFINING THE WAY ENTERPRISES WORK

The technology that sparked the Industrial Revolution ushered in a radical shift in how businesses functioned. Efficiency became the goal, and considerable effort was put into making processes as streamlined and automated as possible, and job descriptions were altered to suit the process. The old method of apprenticeship was set aside, and workers became, in effect, cogs in the machine of industry.

What began with industrial processes in the nineteenth century continued into the twentieth century as the economy became more information-based, and it persists to this day. Technology has fundamentally influenced how we do almost everything. It has moved from the laboratory, to the production shop floor, to a key role in enterprise dynamics, to focusing on employee efficiency and productivity, ultimately crossing over into our personal lives.

We now follow essentially the same workflow model in our daily existence that dominates the workplace. Few of us are able to leave work behind when we go home at the end of the day. For better or worse, technology has largely erased the boundary between our personal and professional lives.

The shape of business and of industry as we now know them can be traced to the dramatic impact of digital technology on the way enterprises function. Most computational innovations were originally used for scientific applications and for automating numeric calculations. Computer programs bore no resemblance to the user-friendly applications that are familiar to us today; rather, the software was highly technical, with narrowly defined scope. Electronic computers were massive, limited, and used only by highly trained specialists. Eventually, of course, computing moved from specialized scientific, military, and engineering uses to play a central role in our daily existence.

Computational innovation led to large commercial applications, which were viewed as a means to automate the enterprise and achieve great advances in speed and efficiency. The idea was to free people from mundane and repetitive tasks to do work that adds value—a theme still used by technology companies today, as computer systems become ever more sophisticated and even "intelligent."

This is the same principle that causes disruption in the workforce. Highly skilled workers, suddenly confronted by technology that makes their skills obsolete, find themselves out of jobs with nowhere to turn. They must find a new niche in order to survive.

As the focus of enterprises turned to overall efficiency improvements in the workplace, production processes were grouped together to achieve scale, then automated to drive greater efficiency and throughput. As noted, this happened in the media industry but it began elsewhere; media companies, facing similar business imperatives, responded in a similar way.

As businesses grew and evolved over time, technology was applied to every process step to make each one more efficient. Tools—first physical, then digital—began to be designed not only to automate the processes but also to facilitate and simplify humans' role in those processes. On an individual level, this led to increased productivity by replacing much of what had been done on paper or through manual labor.

Machining is a good example; before digital technology, precisely machining a part required a high degree of knowledge and manual skill, along with intimate familiarity with complex milling equipment. With the advent of computerized numerically controlled (CNC) manufacturing, parts could be machined with high precision and total repeatability by pressing a button. The skill moved from operating the machine to programming it, and thanks to ever simpler software tools, the degree of required knowledge is less than it once was. Now we're moving on to 3-D printing, and it's so simple that schoolchildren can design and create physical prototypes using inexpensive desktop devices.

As business processes evolved to take advantage of technology, the increasingly automated steps had to be tied together so that each part of the production process could flow into the next more efficiently.

Technology certainly plays a role in that transformation, but the change depends on more than the tools used in the process. Real, meaningful change has to be more fundamental to take advantage of technology and extend across the business.

Consider an early business mainframe computer, such as might have been found at a telephone or electric company. It might have handled customer billing, but much of the rest of the business still relied on manual, paper-based processes. In a situation such as this, technology makes part of the business much more efficient but doesn't really impact the enterprise on a large scale. Media companies are grappling with a similar situation today—outdated processes and economic models that have advanced technology embedded within them, or that can't be readily adapted to take advantage of new technologies, make it difficult to adapt to the new digital landscape.

In industries across the economy, automation technology gradually drove advances in the entire production process. Along the way, enterprise-wide applications began to emerge, ushering in another wave of efficiencies. Businesses were responding to the same imperative: further increasing automation and connecting processes to one another in a drive to improve the efficiency of the whole. Companies began reviewing their entire set of disconnected activities, taking a more holistic view. Areas such as enterprise resource planning, manufacturing process flow, supply chain rationalization, distribution, accounting, invoicing, customer relationship management, and every other facet of the value chain became increasingly dependent on technology, and, as a result, individual productivity skyrocketed.

This transition to technology-based processes represents one of the most significant contributors to extending the labor and productivity gains that began with the Industrial Revolution. However, the shift also fundamentally affected the processes themselves, tending to tie them to the technology in use and thereby hampering the ability of the enterprise to adapt. Each business and manufacturing process that was automated through technology had to be adapted to make the best use of that technology. A workflow that might make sense for a person wasn't necessarily efficient once technology was introduced, and vice versa.

BEYOND PRODUCTIVITY: THE NEED FOR REAL TRANSFORMATION

Today, we're gradually moving to the next level by creating new processes, business models, and connections not possible without digital technology. Instead of taking once-manual processes and attempting to optimize them, we're devising entirely new approaches. The final frontier, yet to be achieved, is to link all the pieces together in a seamless flow that connects the person who conceives a good or service to the person consuming that good or service—shedding the baggage of the past in favor of what's possible today. But we have a long way to go.

Automating a manual process ultimately refocuses the individual on a new, and often more expanded, role. Making tasks faster and easier to accomplish means that people can do more with their time, and get more deeply involved because it's no longer necessary to look to others for assistance.

Think for a moment about what that means for those involved in media, regardless of their place in the ecosystem. For a performer who wants to, say, collaborate with others on a song recording, the process of encoding, transmitting, and hosting a digital file makes it possible to post that video or audio file online for collaborators to access. That kind of self-service production and distribution could never have happened without digitization; a performer who wanted to share a song would have to rely on others to create the finished product and distribute it. That older workflow made sense in the days before the Internet, but it doesn't work as well in today's world.

As with any evolving system, processes and technologies have never been truly static. Just as with people, they must change with the times. Software and business processes are living things, shaped by those who create them. As needs change, a new set of requirements arise, and both the technology and process must adapt or be rendered obsolete.

At any given time, however, people must deal with a specific set of technologies and workflows that are limited by their design, capability, and purpose. It's not as easy to change technology or redefine an established workflow as it is to retrain a person. Building a process around a particular technology is like building a machine: it breeds specialization, leading to processes that are highly optimized, but also rigid and siloed. In response, we naturally organize ourselves along the well-defined lines that technology has imposed upon us. Look in any organization and this can be seen; there are separate departments for different functions, specialized job descriptions, and dedicated technological tools.

The unintended consequence of introducing technology is always a dislocation of talented individuals, who must adapt, retrain, and pursue new careers. It's an old story; journeymen typesetters, for example, were expert in a specialized manual process that was rendered obsolete by desktop publishing software and laser printers. Merely adapting to technological change is no protection; becoming expert in an automated—but still specialized and siloed—process is still a dead end, because that process is ultimately bound to be replaced by something else. Today's workers must be adaptable and able to manage processes, rather than become inextricably embedded within them. The next generation must compete on creativity, ideas, and adaptability rather than expertise in a single skill.

That dislocation is the flip side of technology's benefits. Even as it frees us to do more with our time, to be more creative and productive, it also limits our thinking. When a disruptive technology comes along, we are often slow to recognize how it will ultimately shape us. As a result, there can be disconnects between current reality and what technology makes possible, as people work to sort it all out.

The same thing that has taken place in business and manufacturing has also shaped the media industry. Siloed business processes left over from the pre-digital era persist, but things are changing. Workflows, roles, business models, and even the connection to the consumer are all in a state of flux.

CHAPTER 7

The Rise of the Media Industry

In the future everybody will be famous for fifteen minutes.
—Andy Warhol

While the feedback loop of technology and human expression has existed for millennia, it wasn't until roughly the turn of the twentieth century that the media landscape we recognize today began to take shape, and it was formed largely by technological innovation. Specifically, let's look to the inventions of photography, motion pictures, recorded sound, radio, and television.

Prior to the arrival of these technologies, the only way to experience a performance was in person. News traveled at the speed of the fastest form of transport until the invention of the telegraph.

This revolutionary concept—that media could reach anyone, anywhere, electronically or in prerecorded form—was radically transformative. Suddenly, content creators had new opportunities to share, and make money from, their work. That broke the mold of storytelling forever.

The need to give content creators access to technology and distribute their product created whole new industries. Broadcast networks, movie studios, record companies, and all the professional roles and ancillary businesses that support them became established in an amazingly short time, even by today's standards. An entire media ecosystem sprang into being, seemingly out of thin air.

For the first time, it was possible to experience events as they happened without being there in person, and the impact of those stories rose dramatically. Who could help but be captivated by the live radio broadcast of the *Hindenburg* disaster? It remains riveting to this day. And the idea that a virtuoso performance could be not only heard on the radio but purchased, kept on a shelf, and enjoyed again and again changed the way people thought about entertainment and cultural enrichment.

Storytelling outside of print and live performances became a larger part of popular culture. Movie theaters sprang up even in small towns. Phonographs, radios, and televisions appeared in most households. People organized their schedules around favorite radio and television shows. Going to the movies became a pop culture mainstay. The hunger for new material to fill these channels began to accelerate—a phenomenon that continues to this day even as distribution channels multiply.

As with all technologies, the product (in this case, media content) began to be shaped by the tools used to create it. The length of popular songs was dictated by the space available on recording media—first wax cylinders, and later 78-rpm and 45-rpm discs. That short format had an enduring impact, as pop songs continued to be written to fit into a three- or four-minute time slot long after the technical limits disappeared.

Camera and film technology eventually made wide-screen movies possible, and filmmakers used the new format to frame their shots differently, taking advantage of the new technology to tell their stories in a different way—something that changed the viewing experience when those movies were later shown on squarer 4:3 TV screens. Edits had to be made, with the scene jumping back and forth, or "panning and scanning," to capture characters that were meant to be in the same shot. Inevitably, much of the frame simply had to be cut out. Parts of the story, and subtleties of artistic expression, were lost. Thankfully, with the advent of HDTV and its 16:9 cinema format, that's changed and we can see those films as they were meant to be seen.

The format of the media also became part of the creative expression. At the height of vinyl in the 1970s, albums like the Who's *Tommy* and *Quadrophenia* came out that took advantage of the LP format to tell their story. Even the packaging of albums became part of the story, from the folded-up "newspaper" of Jethro Tull's *Thick as a Brick* to the die-cut sleeve of Led Zeppelin's *Physical Graffiti* and the tongue-in-cheek rolling-paper packet of Cheech & Chong's *Big Bambu*.

AN INDUSTRY SADDLED WITH LEGACY

As noted in the last chapter, with any technology-driven business transformation, it takes time for the people at the center of it to catch up. Compared to the public at large, institutions are notoriously slow to adopt new technologies and models. It's easy to see this in the evolution of the media industry, and it's a particularly acute problem today. The same challenges faced by enterprises in other industries, of processes that were first scaled, then automated and connected—but which never truly acknowledged the disruptive impact of technology—affect the media industry and all those involved in it.

I recall many meetings over the past two decades, in which I tried to convince business leaders of the value of technology that would make their lives better and more efficient. I used example after example of how technology can automate lower-level functions in order to allow more time for human interaction—the best part of our social existence and, arguably, the true source of value. In almost every case, there was resistance and argument as to why the new idea would never work. Those I was talking to were too attached to the familiar and proven. And understandably so; most business-people are inherently risk-averse. True risk takers—people like Elon Musk, the founder of Tesla Motors and SpaceX—are exceedingly rare. Most people need to be convinced and given time to embrace new technologies.

It reminded me of the early days of the ATM; people were so used to traditional banking that they had a hard time recognizing the benefits of access to cash at any time, and many objected to what they perceived as a takeover by mindless technology. They trusted human tellers more than machines, despite the obvious cost, convenience, and accuracy advantages. Banks worked hard to make ATMs seem more "human," even giving them names like "Tammy the Timeless Teller" (yes, that was a real ATM).

Fast-forward to today with the ease of online and mobile banking, instant global cash transfers, automated bill payment, mobile checkout for purchases at the tap of a screen, loan applications with approval via your phone, and yes, even transactional apps that let us deposit paper checks (for those who still use paper) with our phones. Now, we're frustrated by the inefficiency of actually going to a physical bank branch or talking to someone for something that can be done more quickly and easily with technology. Seeing the upside potential takes time.

The baggage of the past always persists; as the saying goes, we're always fighting the last war. Before broadcast, film, and recording, performances were live by definition. So unsurprisingly, in the early days what got broadcast, filmed, and recorded tended to be live performances. This remained true even into the age of television, with many early shows run as if they were stage plays, but with cameras trained on the set. The increased creative freedom afforded by editing, multitrack recording, and the like—the things we now see as an integral part of the creative process—did not arrive right away.

The Tools Advance, Even If the Industry as a Whole Hasn't Caught Up Yet

The technologies of media creation have of course evolved in step with advances in computing, networking, and storage. Digital file formats, microelectronics, and computerized interfaces have made content creation and management so simple that even amateurs can produce material of the highest quality.

Such advancements have had a significant impact on the day-to-day operations of some industries, most notably broadcast news. Information and high-definition imagery flow in constantly over network and satellite connections. Content is readily archived, accessed, edited, and put on air—an absolute necessity in the age of the twenty-four-hour news cycle.

Similar things are happening in the world of education, as learning migrates from the traditional classroom setting to hybrid live/digital instruction and courses taught entirely online. Courseware is progressing from the capture of live lectures for later viewing to increasingly scripted and edited digital content that can tell a more powerful story.

WHO CONTROLS THE CONTENT?

For much of the twentieth century, the business and operational models created at the birth of the new media age persisted. Broadcasting was controlled by radio and television networks. Movies were controlled by the studios. Recorded music was centralized, and the power was in the hands of the record companies. It was, by today's standards, an orderly landscape, based on massive infrastructure investments.

Think about radio and TV broadcasting; it relies on vast numbers of network affiliates, local stations, transmitters, satellites, and a marketing and distribution model optimized to support that infrastructure. Film is similar, with studios heavily dependent on thousands of movie theaters and production facilities. With digital technology now making an end run around all of that infrastructure possible, it's easy to see why media companies in these sectors, forced to adapt to new models while still supporting the legacy infrastructure, are having such a hard time.

This simple, orderly media landscape affected how content was created, how people discovered new material, and how they consumed it. Business controlled the creation and flow of content and money, and content creators had no choice but to go through them. There was relatively little interaction between theaters, television networks, movie companies, and music labels aside from sound track albums, stars who tried to move from one realm to another, and the occasional adaptation of material.

This was a time when media companies could drive demand as they saw fit. Shows like *America's Top 40* and *American Bandstand*, concert tours, television and media appearances of all kinds were tightly controlled. The public was fed what the industry wanted it to see, on the industry's terms.

The economic model that emerged was also very predictable and controlled. The way that media assets were created, distributed, and monetized was well defined and fully optimized by the end of the century—again, it was heavily dependent on the business model, distribution network, and physical infrastructure that had grown up over time.

With relatively few well-defined channels and a finely tuned business model, the industry remained stable and profitable for decades, and considerable money was put into content development. But it was not to last.

CHAPTER 8

The Digital Bombshell

Just keep swimming.

—From *Finding Nemo*

The well-ordered universe of the media industry was thrown into turmoil with the arrival of personal computers, and in particular the Internet. It was a revolution in content, distribution, and business no less significant than the invention of recorded media itself, and the industry is still trying to figure out how to deal with the ramifications.

Digitization allowed the focus to shift from the creation, marketing, and distribution of physical products to the monetization of pure data. It marked the start of a massive disruption that continues to reverberate throughout the industry. Such a sea change takes many years, but there's no denying the direction. Physical media—vinyl, Blu-ray, and CDs (or whatever the future holds), and books—are highly unlikely to disappear, but the writing is on the wall. The future of storytelling is increasingly digital.

THE INCONSTANT WINDS OF DIGITAL CHANGE

The publishing and music sectors of the media industry went through a disruptive digital transformation first, because their content is, from a technology standpoint, simpler. Richer media forms that include more than the written word or a single audio track—such as multimedia productions, video with additional commentary, broadcast television in multiple languages, film in different formats and different versions, and news video with embedded data to facilitate location and retrieval—have had to wait for technology to catch up before it became practical to fully digitize them.

In broadcast and film, the transformation is still ongoing because the barriers to entry are so much higher. For these more complex products, integration of raw material into a cohesive story with reasonable quality and speed of execution is far more complicated, requiring advanced technology, robust data management, reliable and cost-effective storage and retrieval systems, and sophisticated workflows to accomplish. While the tools are less expensive, the process is more far-reaching, intricate, and costly.

The differences in production, distribution, and monetization between different forms of media has the effect of shielding parts of the industry from disruptive change. For example, TV broadcasting as a distribution model is waning as streaming becomes more popular, but the same companies can distribute over digital channels as well—which naturally involves additional investment and complexity since the broadcast infrastructure must still be supported. Nevertheless, it offers a pathway that eases the digital transition and partially protects broadcasters.

Music is more susceptible to disruption because creating and distributing great content can be done more simply. The complexity of creating and distributing something like a film or scripted show means that more people and time are involved. There is still some value in broadcast networks and theater chains—value that has largely evaporated from the music space. These factors create breathing space that eases some of the urgency around digital adaptation, allowing for cash flow that can help position these companies for the future.

The end result of digital transformation is similar regardless of media, however. When new forms of distribution exist that make it cheaper and easier to reach the consumer, and all content is digital, the same kind of changes to the business take place—and those changes are dramatic when compared to the relative stability of media before digitization.

A Storyteller's Perspective: Shaking Up the Economics of a Whole Industry

In just over a century, advances in technology have allowed music to penetrate nearly every aspect of our daily lives. Today, music entertains us, motivates us, inspires us, and comforts us. It is heard in our movies, our television shows, our exercise sessions, our video games, our waiting rooms, our telephones, our houses of worship, our networks, our workplaces, and our politics. Music has truly become the sound track of our lives.

It seems ironic, then, that in recent years the same spirit of relentless technological advance that made the rock star possible is now making it more difficult for her to earn a living doing what she loves. More music is being consumed now and in more ways than ever, but the recorded music industry today stands at about half the revenues it had at the peak of its market at the turn of the twenty-first century.

For most of the recorded music industry's life, fans expressed their passion for music largely through the purchase of the relatively scarce physical record album or single. The music library we owned said as much or more about us and our identity as the clothes we wore, the furniture in our homes, and the books we read. But today music is ubiquitous, more consumed than owned, and it is engaged across a very broad set of our activities—activities that are exploiting the music and underlying intellectual property rights of recorded works in a much wider sense than ever, often in real time, and at an unprecedented pace. But the creator's share of that value, and the share of those who contribute to a creator's success, have been severely diminished. This puts the sound track of our lives at risk.

If we want music to remain such a significant and meaningful part of our lives, we must keep our artists and their ecosystems fed. Recent shifts in consumer technology represent not just unprecedented access to music in today's world, but it also represents a need to redefine how the value between an artist's work and a fan's connection is rewarded. We must begin with a renewed vigor for fair and adequate compensation to the community that makes the sound track of our lives possible. But we must also embrace the same relentless drive behind the technological innovation that made the recorded music star possible to keep her healthy and an intimate part of our everyday lives.

—Barak Moffitt, head of strategic operations at Universal Music Group

STORMING THE MEDIA CASTLE: PUTTING POWER IN THE HANDS OF CONSUMERS

The arrival of computers, connectivity and digital media wasn't the first time that technological disruption created issues for the industry. The legal issues surrounding audiotape recording, and later videotape, had been hashed out in court for years. The industry also had to contend with the introduction and broad acceptance of cable television. In hindsight, it's easy to see the trail that leads from being able to record a movie off of cable and the challenges faced by the film sector today, as the balance between theater attendance and digital consumption continues to shift.

Still, even with these threats, the media industry was able to adhere to existing business models for years. The technology that allowed people to bypass the media companies—audio cassettes and VCRs, for example—didn't deliver the quality that could be had from purchased media. The introduction of audio CDs also helped drive consumption, as people replaced their records with more convenient, higher-quality recordings.

In the 1990s, digital acceleration really got started with MP3 files. People could now create near-perfect copies of audio tracks and share them with relative ease. It wasn't like it is today, of course; the World Wide Web was in its infancy and most connections were by modem.

Still, the arrival of the MP3 format meant music could be heard more easily, and individuals had more choice than ever before. It was also an unprecedented threat to media companies, and piracy ran rampant thanks to file-sharing networks like Napster—an issue that persists today despite advances in digital rights management that have allowed other forms of media to adapt and avoid the same fate. Few could have imagined the destructive effect of digitization on the economic engine of the music industry, the test of our legal system, or its impact on social conscience. It truly was a revolution.

THE iTUNES EFFECT

One of the most important events in modern media history took place in 2001, when Apple introduced the iPod and iTunes. The genius of this new technology was that it fundamentally altered the way music was consumed, and it opened the door to digital distribution of movies and TV as well. The unintended consequences of this move caught the media companies completely off guard, and they've yet to fully recover.

MP3s predated iTunes by a few years, setting the stage for the revolutionary new business model. Consumers had already begun to think about content in a new way; it was about individual tracks rather than albums. iTunes took this to a new level by making each track affordable and very easy to purchase through a slick online business model.

With the entry of Apple into the media universe, the writing was on the wall, though the industry as a whole didn't see it yet. Record companies were still oriented toward CD production and distribution, artists were still focused on creating whole albums, record stores still existed—the entire production, distribution, and monetization infrastructure was still rooted in the models that had worked for nearly a century.

In 2004, unit CD sales were 771 million. By 2015, they'd shrunk to 123 million. Over the same period, unit digital downloads went from 144 million to 1.1 billion.[1] In just a few years, an entire decades-old distribution channel and the monetization model surrounding it effectively collapsed as the result of the new digital business model ushered in by iTunes.

Today, it can be hard to find a good CD selection at retail outlets in the United States, yet the format persists. It is interesting to note that most cars now come with audio input jacks, Bluetooth connectivity, or even full iPod integration as well as CD players. It seems clear that CD players will soon join the cassette deck and the 8-track in the technology graveyard.

Bucking the Downward Trend

Despite the global nature of the digital shift, it's not uniform everywhere. Japan is a good example. In this culture that loves collectibles, CD sales remain strong, and digital sales actually dropped by roughly 60 percent from 2009 to 2014. At the same time, Tower Records—long gone in the U.S. market, having been killed off largely by music downloads and streaming, was doing well in Japan. Surprisingly, in 2014 the Japanese reportedly purchased 85 percent of their music on CDs.[2]

Even today, those legacy ways of thinking about content persist. Arguably, albums are no longer relevant (the small-scale resurgence of vinyl notwithstanding), yet companies still focus on producing them. That's changing, though, with more and more early releases of individual tracks. All it takes is a quick visit to the iTunes Store and a glance at the popularity rankings to see that downloads of individual tracks dwarf album purchases. This is borne out by the data: In 2015, singles accounted for 90 percent of all downloads, some 1 billion. In contrast, just 110 million albums were downloaded—a 9 to 1 ratio.[3]

iTunes meant that it was possible for a person to abandon earlier consumption models. The iPod wasn't the first portable media player (remember the Walkman?) or even the first MP3 player, but it was the first truly compelling alternative total user experience—something that Apple under Steve Jobs fully understood. Forward thinkers among the customer base realized that traditional home stereos weren't really necessary any longer. Even radio became less relevant in the face of the ability to download any track and keep a 1,000-song music library in your pocket. These are the same people who more recently have abandoned traditional media distribution in favor of streaming and consumption on devices such as phones and tablets.

This has led directly to massive fragmentation. Media companies must now support a wide variety of devices, formats, and channels. With the audience now spread out, channels that are costly to support, such as broadcast television and print media, are encountering serious declines in revenue.

THE STREAMING TSUNAMI

iTunes was the first truly different distribution and consumption model to arrive. It wasn't the last, and the original track-centric download model is rapidly being eclipsed by streaming media, just as iTunes disrupted the existing record industry. More importantly, it's not just about music or proprietary models anymore. Now, it's about being able to access all forms of digital media, live or prerecorded, on any device, anywhere, at any time.

As broadband connectivity increased and bandwidth costs dropped, streaming of both audio and video became practical. This, combined with improvements in mobile device technology, meant that TV shows and movies could be watched anywhere with no loss of quality. That launched a whole new set of business models, exemplified by Spotify, Pandora, Hulu, Netflix, and many others. Video gaming, too, has its own online presence through Steam and console-specific gaming networks.

Streaming is the new wave, and in 2015 streaming outpaced digital downloads for the first time.[4] It's easy to see why. Content no longer needs to be purchased and downloaded. Instead, for a monthly fee that's about the same as the download of one album, consumers can buy the right to access a stream and tap into a huge variety of content on demand. Apple responded to the sudden popularity of streaming by launching a service of its own, in part because these competitors have eaten into its market share. They joined a large crowd of players with significant adoption, and even branded artists jumped into the market with their own competitive offerings. As of this writing, the market is crowded and there are no clear leaders. It's possible that just as MP3 players left the Walkman behind and iTunes and the iPod left other MP3 players behind, Apple will become an afterthought in music streaming. History will tell.

Streaming of richer video content has also led to many people "cutting the cord" on their cable service. Hardware manufacturers have recognized the appeal and made it easier to go digital by building HDMI ports into computers and developing technologies like Apple AirPlay for Macs and iOS, Google's Beam for Android, and DLNA support in media players, which allow media streamed to computers and mobile devices to be displayed on televisions.

There's no question that this digital shift is rewriting the rules. Look at new televisions today and you'll find that many no longer come with tuners, but nearly all come with Internet connectivity built in. Most remote controls now have dedicated buttons for Netflix and Amazon. The manufacturers have rightly concluded that customers are rapidly abandoning old models in favor of digital distribution.

DIGITAL DISTRIBUTION HAS CHANGED OUR EXPECTATIONS

Just as with the integration of technology into our daily lives, one of the most fascinating effects of the rise of digital storytelling is its effect on human behavior. In just a few years, our attitudes and expectations—even our understanding of what we're "buying"—have changed dramatically.

In the more traditional media distribution and consumption environment that dominated most of the last century, there were two models:

- Broadcast content would be consumed once, in a well-defined "live" setting (e.g., listening to the radio or watching TV). Generally it was free, paid for by advertising and the sale of broadcast rights. Movies, of course, had a different economic model involving ticket sales, and in the 1970s "pay TV"—what is now called cable—appeared, ushering in the now-familiar concept of subscription services.

- Purchased content would be bought, owned, and kept for reuse later. Once consumers brought home a book, LP, CD, videocassette, or DVD, it was theirs to keep. The consumer paid directly for the product.

Those two models still exist, of course. In broadcasting, major sporting events draw large live audiences and are important sources of revenue. But overall there's been an important, and in many ways subtle, change. The ideas of "ownership" and "broadcast" mean something different than they once did.

In a digital world, what do consumers actually "own?" When a consumer buys and downloads an iTunes track, an Amazon movie, a TV show from Vudu, or a Kindle e-book, that content is not actually owned by the individual. What they're buying is the right to consume it, and they are entirely dependent on the provider to make that content and those rights available on demand. Broadcast content, too, has changed because it's no longer ephemeral; TV shows and movies are readily available for viewing whenever the consumer wishes, and streaming services like market leaders Spotify[5] and Apple Music[6] are filling the niche that was once the exclusive domain of radio.

With on-demand streaming media and DVRs, the concept of what "broadcast" actually means has changed as well. It's no longer necessary to settle down after dinner to watch the evening news when it's all online or recorded on a set-top box. Missing a favorite TV show, or even a whole season, means nothing when it's possible to spend a whole weekend binge-watching on Netflix; it's also now common for hit shows that have gone into syndication, like *The Big Bang Theory*, to be broadcast back-to-back for days at a time. And the value of advertising plummets when skipping all the commercials can be done with the press of a button and consumers can bypass the traditional broadcast networks entirely.

The traditional, ad-supported economic model doesn't work as well as it did in the pre-DVR, pre-streaming days. Digitization actually points a way forward: now, the ability to profile users permits sales of targeted ads and tailored ad insertion that, ideally, can help increase the monetary value of digital content over the long term. Nevertheless, at the moment it's lower than the well-proven broadcast model that provides little consumer information but predictable ad rates.

The nature of the current digital model is making the transition more difficult for heritage media companies. There are costs associated with developing platforms that can service both the legacy business and new digital distribution channels. These costs are not something that new, digital-only enterprises need to deal with.

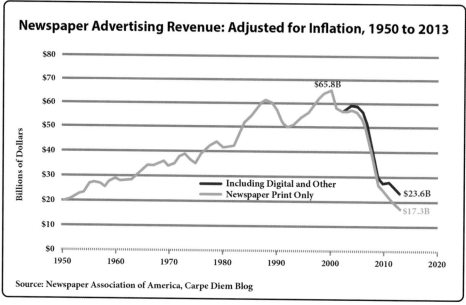

Digitization has had a drastic impact on traditional media, and it's not just because people are choosing online content over older forms. It is in large part the effect of dilution, as consumer attention is spread across more channels.

Making it worse is the fact that the playing field is not level. Digital-only channels are, for the moment, being held to a different standard as the industry undergoes its transition to digital distribution. They are disruptive largely because they are rewarded for aggressive customer acquisition rather than the profit derived from each relationship. The rationale is that the lifetime value of these customers will be very large, once the acquisition costs are past and customer data analytics can be fully leveraged.

This is, of course, unsustainable over the long term, but that is little consolation for established media companies that are losing market share and must answer to their investors. The trick for everyone will be in translating those relationships into ongoing, profitable revenue streams.

Shrinking Revenues: A Problem of Dilution

Digital transformation has resulted in plummeting ad revenue for broadcasters, which is a direct consequence of increasing choice for consumers. Broadcasters and other traditional media platforms, such as newspapers, are caught between a rock and a hard place, forced to fill more distribution channels with more content but getting less revenue from each one. The significant growth in how people can consume media has reduced the viewers on any one channel, which impacts advertising rates.

Having more choice in content and channels has also fragmented audience viewing habits, even as overall consumption rises. As a result, even when a broadcaster has a relative winner, viewership is likely to be spread across a variety of viewing platforms, and the broadcaster is less likely to have as large a share of revenue as it would have when there were only three broadcast networks and no digital choices. The additional distribution allows for access to a greater number of consumers, but the costs are higher and the ad yield is lower. This creates a difficult economic picture.

And when people do consume broadcast content, thanks to DVR technology, they can skip advertisements at will, so there is low engagement. This is why digital distribution channels allow for better prediction of buying behaviors, why cable boxes are increasingly interactive, and why second screens are becoming more important.

But more significant than the impact of recorded broadcast content or content ownership is the shift in consumer purchasing behavior. Streaming, made possible by continuous, reliable broadband connectivity, has changed attitudes on the part of consumers in a way that has far-reaching impact on the media industry.

We no longer think of content as something we buy and own. We're paying subscription fees to walk through the door of a vast warehouse containing anything we can imagine. Once we're there, we're free to choose what we like from near-limitless possibilities. We have traded ownership for convenience and selection.

This shift in attitudes is part of the new "sharing" economy that can be seen in businesses like Airbnb, Zipcar, Uber, and Lyft. Today, easy connections and trust-based business models mean that more and more of us share goods and services to reduce costs. This creates new winners and new losers—it's a different economic model, and traditional businesses, including many media companies, are ill-equipped to take advantage.

The Unique Place of Live Content in Media

Think about another very popular media segment—sports. Sports (and other live events) are one of the few bright spots for all forms of distribution, including broadcast. That's because it is unique content that will only happen once. The media company can control how it's consumed, as long as it controls the rights. It's no wonder that sports licensing has exploded.

The lucrative nature of licensing has amped up the search for new sports to cover, such as mixed martial arts. It's also driven licensing fees sky-high: in 2015, the NFL reportedly achieved a new revenue record of $7.3 billion, a 21 percent increase over 2014. Of that, broadcast networks chipped in $3.1 billion.[7]

Why are broadcasters spending so much? Because 202.3 million unique viewers watched regular-season NFL games in 2014. That's 80 percent of all television homes and 68 percent of potential viewers.[8]

Live-event broadcasting creates new challenges, however. Event video is routinely pirated and posted to services like YouTube, for example. Broadcasters must therefore pour resources into controlling piracy. There's also the massive investment required in enriching the viewing experience, to increase fan engagement. But in the end, the market share and the money it brings in makes the investment worthwhile.

As the music industry has learned, and other sectors are quickly finding out, the implications of near-limitless access to shared content for a fee are profound. Because of instant low-cost (or no-cost) access, each individual work, whether it's a song, a film, a broadcast, or a book, has lower perceived value. We're less likely to want to invest time and money in it. As technology has made it easier for us to connect with stories that move, entertain, and inform us, we have increased our consumption. But at the same time, the surge in choice has made it impractical to spend more time exploring any one piece of content.

Consumers expect endless selection and constant development of new content that they can consume on when, where, and how they choose. There's also an expectation of "free," which makes it harder to convince people to part with their money or willingly make the traditional tradeoff between exposure to advertising and the content they want. Combined with a now-fragmented digital landscape, this new attitude has added enormous complexity to the task facing media companies. These are some of the key factors at the root of how the industry works today, and they present challenges we all face.

PART 3

Why Things Work the Way They Do— or Not

CHAPTER 9

Who's Driving the Bus? Look in the Mirror

I'll have what she's having.
—From *When Harry Met Sally*

As technological innovation accelerates, so too does the rate of adoption. In an era where every aspect of our lives is being reengineered and the acceptance of technology as a key enabler has increased, we are seeing radical shifts in many industries. The media landscape is no different.

Consumers don't want to be constrained by static viewing times on devices attached to the wall or sitting on a table. Why can't they see what they want, when they want? As tools and technologies have made this a reality, we are seeing a rapid transition in consumer demand and behavior. Technology itself is simply the enabler.

What we as consumers—and humans—are looking for are stories that connect us, and if we can have freedom of choice in where, when, and how we consume those stories at a reasonable cost, adoption rates go up. We've seen prior technologies fail miserably for a variety of reasons, from lack of simplicity or ubiquity to cost and complexity to connectivity issues.

For the community at large, there's a complex combination of reasons behind the adoption of new technologies. Improvements in connectivity and processing speeds have opened the door to innovation in our personal lives, much as they have for decades in the corporate world. For major media companies, the ability to adjust is a function of economic pressure and internal cultural barriers. The more intense the economic pressure, the more incentive to break past habits out of necessity. It's cultural adaptation that ultimately drives adoption rates as consumers embrace the latest innovations.

The rate of change is staggering and costly. Investment is made in a technology or service, only to have it collapse soon after as something new comes along. That affects manufacturers, retailers, and consumers just as much as it does media companies. The history of technology is littered with failed ideas that consumed massive amounts of capital. VHS vs. Betamax, DVD-R vs.

Industry's Ability to Adapt to Change

	Change happens slowly Participants adjust opportunistically **Automakers** **Apparel**	Change happens fast Participants adjust and thrive **Social networks** **Consumer electronics**
Ability of Culture to Adapt	Change happens slowly Participants adjust slowly **Agriculture** **Mining**	Change happens fast Participants struggle to adjust **Record Labels** **Newspaper publishers**

Economic Pressures →

Blu-ray, iPod vs. Zune, 3-D television—the wasted money and effort is incredible. And leading technology companies are not immune. Remember Apple's Newton?

As noted earlier, technological innovations are changing our behavior. Not long ago, televisions and stereos were centerpieces of the American living room. But now, more and more people are finding them of less value, and they're abandoning these technologies in favor of computers and mobile devices. For many, the television has become a part of the media hardware suite, serving as a large monitor for streaming content or a second screen.

The same shift away from tradition goes for services. Why pay for cable when Netflix and Hulu have enough content to occupy a person 24/7 for the rest of their life? Why pay for content when a tailored playlist can be built in YouTube? Why download one track when you can subscribe to a streaming service and instantly access millions?

Building Disruption Into the Business Model

As HDTV and video streaming became established, more and more consumers abandoned old consumption models. Film and television companies responded to this new threat by altering the terms on which they compete.

With less differentiation between the theater experience and watching a movie at home, fewer people were going to the multiplex. Hollywood answered by making ever more spectacular blockbusters—movies that look better on big screens—and doubling down on audio and film technology. Formats like IMAX 3D and DTS audio have transformed the moviegoing experience, drawing people back into theaters. More recently, with rich media content available via broadband, studios are supplementing the theater experience with online content like multimedia websites, featurettes, teaser videos, extended trailers, and behind-the-scenes content. Without the disruptive threat of digital distribution and streaming video, these improvements would arguably never have happened.

In the world of television, services like Hulu, Amazon, and Netflix began to cut into cable TV subscriptions as people found that there were alternatives to paying for hundreds of channels, yet only watching a handful. In this case, the response was to give people a reason to tune in by greatly improving the quality of programming, with shows like *The Sopranos, Mad Men, Breaking Bad,* and *Game of Thrones* available only on cable. For viewers, the disruption brought by technology had the welcome effect of creating a new golden age of television.

For years, industries of all kinds have pursued what's been seen as a key promise of digitization: the ability to achieve tailored delivery to each user. Like so many others, in the 1990s I used the term "mass customization," when talking about the benefits of digitizing the delivery of content, as a way to tailor specific choices to customers based upon their user profiles. The thought was that greater availability and connectivity would ultimately lead to a kind of nirvana, where everyone could get exactly what they want when they want it.

A few things have happened since then:

- First, the tools to learn more about your preferences have gotten dramatically better. Using sophisticated algorithms, data collection, and analytics, it's much easier for a business to know a person's preferences. The way content is created and managed—with digital media carrying embedded information that allows for efficient cataloging, search, and retrieval—now enables companies to deliver much more accurate choices to the user. Also, because the ads that support content delivery can be profiled, the likelihood of delivering the right content at a lower price increases.

- Second, the acceptance of such recommendations by consumers has increased dramatically. Consumers have shifted from a fear of "Big Brother" knowing too much to acceptance of the idea that suggestions which make life simpler and better are a good thing despite the fact that digital fraud and scams continue to be serious issues. People are increasingly willing to trade their usage data and personal information to gain perceived benefits. If a company actually does recommend the things the consumer wants and it saves time and money, all well and good—but only if that preference information is used to make the individual's life better and not for nefarious reasons.

- Third, there is so much content now available that branded and trusted sources are needed to recommend the discovery of new stories to consume. For example, I'm not sure which of the myriad new songs coming out I might want to listen to, so I'll rely on what a major music label produces or what most people like in a category because I don't have time to sift through that many songs.

The Instant Customization Engine

Audiences can have a substantial influence on content. By connecting creative professionals directly to the people who consume their work, the creative process can become more organic and take on a life of its own. Online community members can have a hand in shaping the direction of content, thus giving them the opportunity to become emotionally invested in it.

If you're writing short stories or posting music or videos online, for instance, with the right interactive platform people who enjoy the type of content you create could instantly tell you what they like or dislike, arming you with information about what kinds of material would satisfy their needs and desires. If you're a blogger, you could get immediate, real-time feedback from your readers on what you've written. They could tell you what they care about, and that would inform what you write about next. Musicians could get suggestions from their fans about which version of a song they prefer or whether a song is worthy enough to be included on an album. Fans could even submit potential cover art or song ideas. In fact, some musicians have been working this way for years.

If you're a content creator, what you do with your audience's feedback is up to you. You don't have to conform to your community's suggestions, but the choice is there if you want it. You could decide to be provocative and create something that's very different from what your fans expect, or you could deliver a product that they're all but guaranteed to support. It's a new dimension to storytelling that comes from our ability to connect with one another anytime, anywhere.

THE PARADOX OF ENDLESS CHOICE

Mass customization has long been a glowing promise of the digital revolution. The idea is compelling: once everything is digitized, tracked, and tagged so that we can easily find it, once we've established a digital persona and history (willingly or not), tailored content based on our profiles can be fed directly to us. Our own actions result in increasingly focused targeting.

This is now coming to pass, partly because technology has gotten better at not only tracking what we think we like, but at predicting what we might like based on what we've purchased, clicked on, lingered over, or interacted with in some way—who we know or follow, where we go online, and what we search for. Even the physical locations we choose to visit are becoming part of our profile. Leaving these digital footprints is inevitable, given that the vast array of choices forces us to filter what we consume.

With consumers clamoring for more content, more choice, and more convenience, media companies must sink enormous amounts of money into capturing a share of the exploding market by pumping out more and more content, for more channels and more devices.

But faced with so many choices, consumers can't keep up. The average time U.S. adults are exposed to rich electronic media via television, radio, and digital platforms rose from 445 minutes in 2005 to 666 minutes in 2015—an incredible increase of 50 percent.[1] There's simply too much to consume and too many channels—so much variety that choice backfires. The degree of choice is so great and the catalog is so vast that the chances of any individual work, whether it's a song, a film, or a new TV show, rising above the noise are very small indeed.

Despite the greater choice and tailored offerings that analytics offer, consumption patterns have become more concentrated. Collectively we watch and listen to a smaller proportion of available content—that which is defined by mass-market appeal.

This highlights another point: we want shared experiences. As humans, we naturally gravitate to the things that appeal to us all. The opinions of others matter to us, so there's a tendency to favor what's popular.

We are drowning in content and so short of time and attention that the delight of discovering something new is harder and harder to come by. As a result, consumers increasingly rely on curated sources, paradoxically giving up the choice they desire so much in the interest of convenience. We have become a society focused on "what's trending" rather than the content itself, willing to be led to what's deemed worthwhile by others rather than choosing for ourselves.

Sources that guide consumers to content take many forms. Websites like rottentomatoes.com offer crowd-sourced movie and television reviews; there are tightly focused streaming "radio" stations on Sirius XM and Apple Music; and merchants like Amazon use sophisticated analytics and pattern-recognition algorithms to guide us to content we might like. Netflix, Amazon, and Hulu all change their lineups regularly, guiding subscribers to new content. Even such unlikely outlets as NPR are getting into the act; there's a web page with a playlist of 100 "must-hear" songs from the South by Southwest festival, intended to introduce listeners to new bands.

This desire to spend less time and effort choosing content is part of what's driving the rise of streaming. Just as MP3s, file sharing, and iTunes transformed media consumption and changed the face of the industry, streaming is doing it again; people are now used to having targeted content delivered to them rather than having to go out and find it. The proliferation of choice makes competition that much harder, even as overall consumption rises. With only so much consumer time and attention available, companies are challenged to make any headway. There's been a diffusion of consumption, with more and more outlets, formats, and titles all competing for the same eyes and ears, driven by the need to capture market share and demonstrate growth even at the expense of profitability.

The new battleground is the consumer touch point. With less control over how people encounter new media, companies and content creators must seize every conceivable opportunity to expose the public to their product. A consumer's first exposure to a song or artist might be in a commercial, during the closing credits of a movie, in a video game, or as part of the sound track of a television show. The old TV broadcast model of fall show introductions and summer reruns has given way to continuous introduction of new content, so at any given moment there's always something fresh. And all of this is in addition to the traditional promotional appearances on TV talk shows and at public functions, press interviews, and all the rest.

Sadly, ceding choice to third parties only serves to reinforce an imbalance in investment on the part of media companies that hurts most content creators. Money and resources are pumped into promoting a few mega-hits and superstars, who then tend to dominate the curated sources that consumers trust at the expense of those lesser known. The proliferation of choice is paradoxically eroding the rich diversity of high-quality content that should exist.

CHAPTER 10

Why the Industry Is Broken: A Tale of Unintended Consequences

Do or do not, there is no try.

—From *Star Wars*

The extraordinary difficulty of competing in the current environment has driven media companies in directions that they never anticipated. They must produce more content than ever before and support more distribution choices in addition to their existing infrastructure and business models, but their budgets aren't growing fast enough because revenues can't keep up with new business requirements.

THE FORCES DRIVING THE INDUSTRY TODAY

Several large-scale trends are having a dramatic and ongoing impact on the economics of the media business. These are creating powerful driving forces and barriers for media companies across the spectrum, from music to film to broadcast, gaming, and beyond.

Trend #1: Concentration of Consumer Choice

More choices have led to more concentrated consumption, not less as might be expected. Over the long term, that has a corrosive effect. Concentration at the top means that the money goes to those most likely to succeed. That in turn means fewer artists will make it, and those that try to break through will earn less unless they're at the very top. This will eventually lead to lower quality and less choice of new content.

That's not the way it was supposed to be. Earlier, we discussed the mass customization concept: in theory, if we could just digitize all existing and new content and distribute it according to consumer preference, we would see a lower concentration of content consumption. More choice should lead to broader consumption (and more revenue) because companies could track and readily respond to consumer tastes even if they didn't match what was most popular.

The logic was that the major labels, production studios, and media houses that controlled distribution and intellectual property rights would no longer need to work as hard to drive demand. Without customization, consumers didn't have a low-cost way to consume what they wanted when they wanted. People either watched and listened to the choices that the industry created for them, or they would have to go on a long, strange hunt for esoteric titles in the odd music store, club, indie film festival, or art house. Mass customization would supposedly make that unnecessary and allow consumers to find all that they love with ease.

But in fact, the digitization of content has had the opposite effect. As choice proliferated, it became overwhelming, and unless people were intensely interested and engaged, they couldn't afford the time and effort to filter the dramatic increase in choices. As noted earlier, the result is that consumers look for filters to decide what to watch or listen to; the taste of others trumps that much-vaunted personal tailoring.

Companies making selections for us using proven techniques for identifying the "best" actors, directors, musicians, and stories turned out to have real value. They fill the role of trusted brands that can help us decide what's worth consuming. In addition, digitization and connectivity tools have allowed consumers to more easily understand what is most popular, as consumption patterns create a crowd consensus: rather than filter ourselves, we gravitate toward the most popular movies, TV shows, and music. As a result, there is actually more concentration, not less, despite a dramatic increase in choice.

Trend #2: Shift in Investments to Distribution and Monetization

At the same time as there is more concentration and rapid increases in both content creation and consumption, there's been a much more dramatic proliferation of digital formats, channels and devices through which to consume content. In order for the industry to adapt, compete, and maintain stable profits, significant investment in these newer models is necessary. That money must come from somewhere else.

That's forced a large-scale shift in budgets to support these areas. The good news is that these new ways of connecting give the media industry access to a larger audience all around the world. The bad news is, the revenue from new digital channels is much lower than that obtained from broadcast and other traditional forms of distribution. Making matters worse is the emphasis by digital-only media disruptors on consumer acquisition rather than the profit that will eventually be required to maintain the distribution channel. Media companies must choose where to spend their limited money in the face of this reality.

As a result, while the importance of creating better content is recognized, there is greater pressure to monetize that content and support all these new channels and platforms. Even if media companies wanted to hold on as long as they could to traditional distribution channels where profits are greater, they couldn't. Depending on the geographic region, consumers have an increasing number of alternative content and consumption choices, and little reason to stay with the old channels.

To participate in the marketplace, media companies either need to adapt by offering similar distribution options or risk being reduced to irrelevancy. As this painful and delicate transition away from the old model advances, companies must manage a complicated shift from the tools, infrastructure, organization, and people dedicated to traditional channels toward a profile that better supports the new model. This naturally moves money away from creative tools to the distribution and monetization tools.

Think about it. There is more pressure than ever to both create more at a lower cost and automate the entire media workflow. If you have a small increase in overall spending, and new digital distribution and monetization tool investment is growing at a much faster rate, something has to give. Usually, it's creative and infrastructure budgets, along with investment in more established and profitable distribution models, that suffer.

The movement of resources from content creation to monetization is made worse by the fact that new digital distribution models, such as streaming, are less mature and less profitable. And there are more of them, requiring media companies to spread budgets more thinly.

Trend #3: Lack of Tools to Support New Business Models

Many of the companies that support the media industry face the same dilemma as their customers. Walk the halls of industry trade shows and events, and it's easy to see. Many software, hardware, and service providers created tools for a different time and a different place, and they have found it difficult to move beyond those legacy investments.

The media technology landscape is littered with too many vendors chasing too few dollars, with proprietary, siloed tools designed for a time when business models were different. Some romantically hold on to the past, hoping that someday we'll return to a simpler time in which a series of disconnected tools still works and can be supported by what is now an outdated economic model. New applications to replace these technologies don't need to come from the same players, or even be hardware-based; media companies can, in many cases, simply move to pure-play online providers. But the marketplace has yet to mature.

Today, most legacy tools are ill-suited for the digital reality that is upon us, and gone are the days of creating new products that only work in proprietary formats that make it costly and difficult to connect. The situation has reached a boiling point, and the industry has been forced to turn to unproven, early-stage technologies that don't scale and lack the ability to deal with the complexity of the industry. Eventually, these tools will give way to a more efficient and collaborative approach to media production, but we're not there yet.

THE DILEMMA FACING MEDIA COMPANIES

While the transition to a more digitized world is occurring, media companies must continue to compete and win. Some of their challenges date back to the origin of the media business itself—content, for example, is still king. But there are many new issues to contend with.

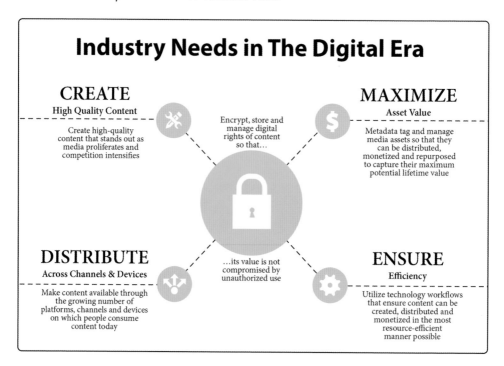

The business imperatives that media companies face as they shift to increasingly digital business models are multifaceted but on the whole straightforward. These enterprises must:

- **Create great content**—Over the past decade, the broader availability of low-cost, high-quality professional tools has allowed many more people to tell their story. However, the dramatic rise in content has also made it harder to be heard, putting additional pressure on creating the very best content. Whether it's a better news story to inform, a scripted show or game to entertain, a major motion picture, or professional music meant to inspire, the competition to be heard is more severe than ever. The need to work efficiently with the best talent anywhere in the world to create the best sound or story has intensified.

- **Make the content available to more channels and devices**—Rising even faster than the volume of content itself is the number of ways in which audiences expect to consume it. Stories can (and need to) be found via traditional outlets, such as movie theaters, broadcast networks, radio, or downloaded files, but increasingly that content must be made available in multiple formats, on a wide variety of devices and digital channels, each with varying data structures, requiring greater investment for the same piece of content to reach the audience. As expectations rise for greater choice on how people consume content, the cost and complexity of distribution has gone up. The industry now has more ways to connect with almost every community on the planet; however, the economic model for sustaining these formats has yet to prove itself.

- **Optimize the lifetime value of the content**—While many artists create content for the joy of being heard, economically supporting that passion has become more complicated than ever. If media companies find the winner that connects with audiences, they must work harder to optimize the value so that they can continue to sustain bringing more content to the market. This means making sure that any part of the content can be reused easily, that it can be accessed anytime anywhere quickly and inexpensively, that the rights to different parts of the content can be identified and used easily, that it can be made available in multiple formats at a low cost, and that it can be available immediately at any time. Optimizing lifetime value also means more intimate, more intense, and longer engagement with audiences; it's the human connection that drives consumption. Here, immersive storytelling is playing an increasing role, starting with gaming, concerts, and sporting events.

- **Do everything more efficiently**—As described earlier, although the overall spending is increasing, it's not keeping pace with the amount of content and distribution channels that consumers expect to enjoy. In addition, the shift to digital channels and economic models is putting tremendous pressure on the workflow of media operations. No matter where or how you participate, you're feeling increasing pressure to do more with less. The hunger for new technologies to connect all the pieces, make production more efficient, and integrate processes is accelerating.
- **Make it secure**—Security has always been a concern, but today it's becoming an even larger issue. Just as in other industries and in our personal lives, as we increasingly rely on digital connections we are exposed to new security issues. These security concerns vary widely. News organizations and their networks that want to get the story out as quickly and easily as possible are prime targets for certain groups ready and able to cause harm because they don't like the stories, or

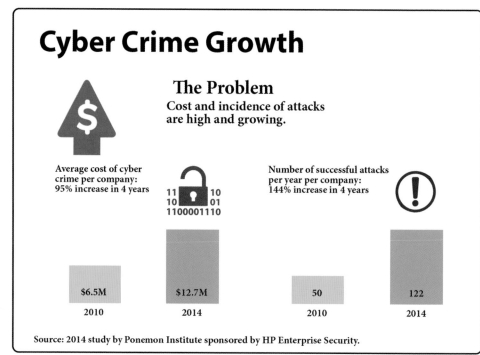

Cyber Crime Growth

The Problem
Cost and incidence of attacks are high and growing.

Average cost of cyber crime per company: 95% increase in 4 years

11 10
10 01
1100001110

$6.5M — 2010
$12.7M — 2014

Number of successful attacks per year per company: 144% increase in 4 years

50 — 2010
122 — 2014

Source: 2014 study by Ponemon Institute sponsored by HP Enterprise Security.

want to find out who is writing them, or track down the sources for retaliation. Once off-limits, journalists are now at great risk; in 2013, 66 were murdered around the world, and in 2014, 137 were abducted, with many still held years later.[1] Major film studios want to ensure that the next blockbuster doesn't get released to the public in an uncontrolled way, placing substantial ticket revenue and other monetary opportunities at risk. Without those revenue sources, the studios couldn't sustain creating new stories and bringing them to market. For a music company or individual artist, piracy represents a direct and fundamental threat to their livelihood. Every illicit track download or unrecognized playback royalty is a straight loss.

A Storyteller's Perspective: The Multiple-Format Nightmare

Media is now ubiquitous in terms of its location, timing, and medium for display, and the variety of devices is endless and ever changing. Large, wide-aspect, fixed screens can include plasma, LCD, quantum-dot, and OLED technologies. Handheld devices have generally narrower aspect ratios and any number of sizes and display technologies.

So how is the artistic intent of content affected by different display mediums? Perhaps the largest variable confronting the media artist is aspect ratio. With originating cinema aspect ratios being 21:9 or wider, television at 16:9, and tablets tending to be more square, while content increasingly is captured and displayed vertically on cell phones, the challenge to preserve the original artistic intent is immense.

Different display technologies also beget different viewing habits. Larger screen sizes generally mean longer viewing times. As we see the increasing prevalence of smaller screens, we also see more content viewed with very short run times.

Production techniques must now not only accommodate current consumption methods but also anticipate an otherwise unpredictable future of media displays. Today, artists have worked in particular mediums, such as film or television, and subsequent treatments have been employed to produce new media versions. As the media landscape changes, content creators will need to interface more directly with technology to ensure that their artistic intent is preserved as it is translated to different mediums.

Large media organizations are leading the charge to formats like SMPTE IMF, allowing content to be marked with metadata that preserves or interprets artistic intent as these varied transformations occur. The industry is waking up to the new relationship between the creative process and technology.

—Paul Stechly, ACA leader, Applied Electronics

THE FALLOUT: MONEY RISES TO THE TOP

Since consumer consumption patterns have led to greater concentration, those that win, win big, and they're making it harder for unrecognized artists to make it.

It took some time for this concentration to take place. Early in the shift toward digitization the industry took a portfolio approach. There was more content variety, with a mix of smaller, unknown, indie-related projects balanced by some large "tent pole" projects. That model has eroded, as the consumption patterns have shifted to proven stories and storytellers. As a result, the smaller projects are being crowded out by larger projects from proven players to ensure they are on the right end of the content consumption curve.

Media companies, finding that the "long tail" of available content has less value due to tighter concentration, have been forced to focus their investments. The result is more hurdles for anyone trying to break into the business.

It takes so much money and effort to get attention in an environment of endless choice that for every Taylor Swift or Beyoncé, there are myriad talented storytellers who cannot get any traction because the smartest move for a media company is to reduce risk by supporting a known success.

At the same time, the increasing adoption of low-margin digital channels makes participation in the marketplace less profitable for content creators. To make matters worse, in some segments piracy is still a major issue, which further damages their ability to make a living. The biggest losers are the individual artists—although everyone loses when content is stolen. Content creators obviously lose because they're not being compensated for their hard work. Media companies lose because there's less money to invest in new, high-quality content and better customer experiences. Consumers lose too, because they're not supporting the storytellers that create the content they love, and without that support those artists may have to leave the stage.

This combination of greater concentration in the face of more choices and the increased use of less profitable digital channels has had a significant negative impact on traditional media companies and the content creators who rely on them. The biggest winners in the game are digital distributors and digital channel providers who aren't burdened with the legacy models and infrastructure that the older companies must support. As we've seen with the evolution of the World Wide Web, there is a higher value potential placed on digital channels. In the dot-com bust, many of the early pioneers came crashing down and never recovered when their funding dried up and profits were nonexistent.

Forward-looking digital distributors in this wave recognize this and are moving into the content creation side. Nontraditional players like Netflix are producing some of the best programming. When the dust settles, those that get it right are positioned to become media powerhouses in their own right.

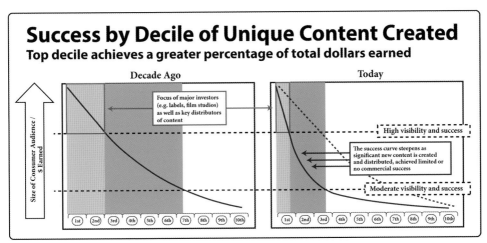

Ten years ago, new content stood a better-than-even chance of at least moderate success. But with increased filtering by consumers and intense concentration on top-earning properties by media companies, it's harder to see daylight. This creates a vicious cycle that discourages content creators, who stand little chance of making it.[2]

This fallout from concentration is reflected in the real world. Take a look at box-office success for new movies over the past twenty years. Earlier we observed that even as content proliferates, audiences driven by mass-market appeal tend to focus on less of what's out there. The data proves this out.

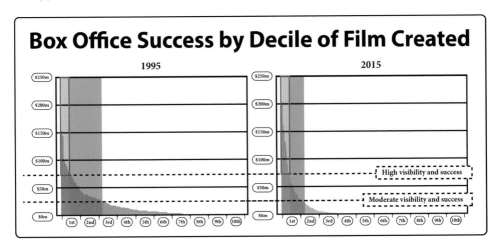

At the left end of the charts are the most successful and popular movies of the year. In 1995, 37 percent of the movies released made up 90 percent of total gross domestic revenue. By 2015, a much smaller percentage was likely to achieve the same; in that year, only 12 percent of all movies released generated 90 percent of total gross domestic revenue.[3]

Put another way, in 1995, 90 percent of box office proceeds came from 37 percent of the movies in distribution. In 2015, 12 percent of the movies in distribution accounted for 90 percent of revenue. In short, only the biggest hits are drawing audiences today.

What does this mean for a movie studio? To make any money, all the backing has to go to blockbusters that stand a reasonable chance of filling theater seats during those critical first few weekends. It's not only the initial box office that matters; the incremental revenue from a known and successful movie once the film is out of theaters is substantially higher. The so-called smaller or indie films are less profitable over both the short and long term. So, even though more of these movies are being made, less funding is available to make them successful, and they're less likely to be distributed nationwide. There's a reason why all the theaters in a given area seem to be showing the same movies, and this is it.

That's bad news for up-and-coming filmmakers, who may find a warm reception and great success at film festivals like Sundance or Cannes but are unable to break through to become commercially viable. The economic incentive to take a chance is low, making for intense competition for funding.

For moviegoers, it means that there's actually *less* choice of new content that might make it worthwhile to spend money on a movie ticket. By the third weekend, there are likely to be only a handful of patrons in any given showing, and the film won't be in theaters for very long, if it ever makes it to the multiplex at all.

A similar situation holds for TV. According to media blog REDEF, in 2000, approximately 90 percent of original scripted television series made it to a second season. By 2014, that number was about 50 percent.[4] That's despite a compound annual growth rate of 14 percent in scripted TV series over the past five years.[5]

There's a lot more churn now, as networks concentrate on more successful shows and are very quick to pull the plug on those with low ratings. In 2015, CBS canceled *Angel from Hell* after only five episodes had aired. Meanwhile, evergreen franchises like *Survivor* and *NCIS* are renewed year after year and spawn multiple spin-off series. This is an example of how media companies,

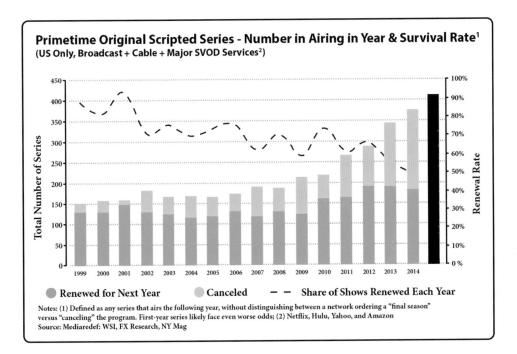

Primetime Original Scripted Series - Number in Airing in Year & Survival Rate[1]
(US Only, Broadcast + Cable + Major SVOD Services[2])

● Renewed for Next Year   ● Canceled   – – Share of Shows Renewed Each Year

Notes: (1) Defined as any series that airs the following year, without distinguishing between a network ordering a "final season" versus "canceling" the program. First-year series likely face even worse odds; (2) Netflix, Hulu, Yahoo, and Amazon
Source: Mediaredef: WSI, FX Research, NY Mag

in the never-ending drive to keep revenue flowing, act conservatively and devote their resources to proven properties. There's not much appetite for risk, so the formula is followed. That makes it harder for truly new ideas to find their way to audiences.

The music industry is no different. According to 2013's *Next Big Sound State of the Industry Report*, more than 90 percent of all artists are undiscovered, and popularity is proportional to exposure—in other words, the larger the following already is, the more new followers the artist will gain.[6] Only 1 percent or so of artists rise to "mainstream" or "mega" status, and roughly 80 percent

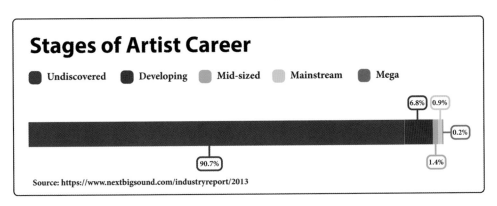

Stages of Artist Career

● Undiscovered   ● Developing   ● Mid-sized   ● Mainstream   ● Mega

6.8%   0.9%

0.2%

90.7%

1.4%

Source: https://www.nextbigsound.com/industryreport/2013

of the artists that the report tracked got less than one Facebook page like per day. Without support, it's almost impossible to get a break. But once again, look at it from the point of view of the record label. Where is the best place to put your money?

It's a situation worthy of *Alice's Adventures in Wonderland*. There's more content than ever, more consumption than ever, more choices in how to discover and consume new material . . . yet more focus on a few mega-hits than ever, which will ultimately lead to *less* variety, as those who can't see the light of day leave the game entirely.

THE SLOW DEATH OF GREAT CONTENT

There's one statistic that I find especially troubling. In 2015, streaming of existing songs ("catalog" content) outstripped new music for the first time, and only 30 percent of the traffic was new material, according to *Billboard*.[7] Much of this can be attributed to the shift away from downloaded content. On-demand streaming makes it easier and less expensive for consumers to access the full catalog without having to make an additional purchase. In other words, as purchases fall and streaming increases, new music is losing market share.

But in my view, it's not just about the shift in distribution model. It's also a reflection of something deeper and more disturbing. People are consuming more catalog content because they aren't finding value in new content—they prefer material they already know.

After all, the same streaming service can deliver new content as readily as catalog content, so there must be a reason why the traditional 50/50 split between catalog and new releases is changing. In short, from the consumer's perspective, the quality of new content is not up to the standards of what came before. It's beginning to look like the corrosive effect of low investment in content creation is starting to appear. By concentrating on the top end, media companies are allowing up-and-coming talent to wither on the vine. Consumers simply are not able to find and enjoy new content with which they truly connect. The exceptions, of course, are the blockbuster hits from major artists that we all know and love. These are the properties that media companies pour resources into.

Part of the problem is that in the current environment, new artists have a harder time establishing and developing their careers. There have always been one-hit wonders, but today even truly talented acts have tremendous difficulty gaining traction and may disappear before the public has a real chance to discover them. This is an unintended consequence of the 40 percent reduction in artist pay that's occurred as distribution models have shifted to digital and streaming and budgets have gone to monetization of proven properties. The crushingly low level of compensation forces artists to make decisions earlier about whether they can make a sustainable living doing what they love. Many play just to be heard, but at some point, economic reality sets in and they're forced to move on.

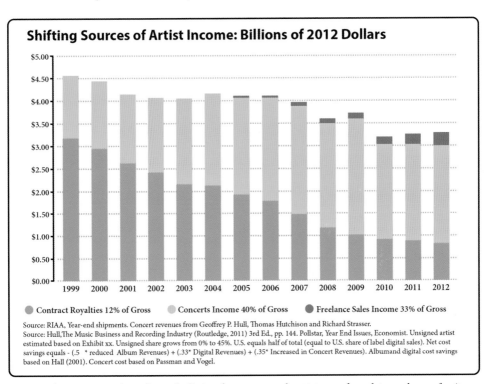

Shifting Sources of Artist Income: Billions of 2012 Dollars

Source: RIAA, Year-end shipments. Concert revenues from Geoffrey P. Hull, Thomas Hutchison and Richard Strasser.
Source: Hull, The Music Business and Recording Industry (Routledge, 2011) 3rd Ed., pp. 144. Pollstar, Year End Issues, Economist. Unsigned artist estimated based on Exhibit xx. Unsigned share grows from 0% to 45%. U.S. equals half of total (equal to U.S. share of label digital sales). Net cost savings equals - (.5 * reduced Album Revenues) + (.33* Digital Revenues) + (.35* Increased in Concert Revenues). Album and digital cost savings based on Hall (2001). Concert cost based on Passman and Vogel.

Royalty payments have been declining for years, and artists are forced to make up for it with concerts and freelance income—but even that isn't enough.

In the short term, the industry has been riding a wave of technological change that's supported consumption, from physical formats to digital, and from download to streaming. The growth bet right now is on improving the streaming experience, but the revenue model isn't working very well yet, especially for the artists. Streaming margins are so thin that a major industry shake-up is in the offing; although enterprise values can be high, the economics are unproven.

More important over the long term, however, is the quality issue. Eventually the failure to invest sufficiently in the next generation of content is going to come home to roost. For media companies, the shift in interest toward older material is a warning sign—broaden the base, invest in quality content, and make it worthwhile to be a storyteller, or face a future of shrinking revenue and market share.

CHAPTER 11

Where We Stand Today

'Cause it's a bittersweet symphony, this life.

—The Verve

The digital revolution that started near the turn of the twenty-first century continues, and it's landed us in an interesting place. The technology-driven democratization that started with consumption in the twentieth century with the introduction of recorded and broadcast media has, in this century, extended to creation and distribution.

Thanks to easy-to-use, inexpensive tools and ready connectivity, more content is being created and consumed than ever before. The software, hardware, and online technologies available for video and audio production at the consumer level are easily capable of producing professional-level results. Even higher-end solutions are more affordable than ever, with lower prices and new subscription models that require no large up-front investment, mirroring the ongoing trend in media consumption.

For example, Avid Media Composer, one of the most popular and powerful tools for studio film and television editing, cost more than $100,000 in 1989. Today, it's $1,299 to purchase and as low as $49.99 a month for a one-year subscription in the cloud—and thanks to advances in computing, it performs better and is easier to use. Also, for those who want to discover digital editing, a free version called Media Composer First has been announced so that more people can tell their story. Media Composer is one of the most important and widely used products in the industry, with major educational institutions around the world offering certification courses to prepare their students for careers in media. According to PayScale, which has compiled the world's largest database of 54 million individual salary profiles, the average salary for video editors with Avid skills is 44 percent higher than the average salary for all video editors.[1] Media Composer was used in the production of each of the top-ten films released domestically in 2015. These films generated approximately 35 percent of U.S. box office film revenue.[2] That's the kind of positive economic impact a piece of technology can have on the media industry and the people who are part of it.

This trend toward lower prices and subscription-based business models extends across the industry. Adobe Premiere, for example, was offered as a stand-alone product in 2008 for $799 and is now included in the Adobe Creative Cloud suite for $49.99 a month for a one-year subscription—a price that nearly anyone can afford. Improved accessibility has driven wider acceptance of tools like these, and they are now a standard part of the filmmaker's tool kit, making a good entry point for aspiring creative professionals, helping them create content able to win major awards. In fact, such tools are very popular with indie filmmakers and were used in the production of 175 of the films at the 2016 Sundance Film Festival—an increase of 143 percent over 2015.[3]

A Storyteller's Perspective: Extending Opportunities to Create and Tell Stories

As the author of six book titles on Pro Tools and a college professor in a commercial music program, I am passionate about teaching media-related software and enhancing students' opportunities to learn. The changes that Avid has made with Pro Tools 12 have had a tremendous impact on who has the opportunity to master the software and how they can realize their creative aspirations.

In years past, many of my students did not have direct access to Pro Tools software outside of the classroom or lab environment. This was particularly true for students from underprivileged backgrounds or low-income families— they simply could not afford to purchase the software. This lack of access directly impacted their ability to learn and their ability to utilize Pro Tools for their own musical and storytelling endeavors.

The software-subscription model that was introduced with Pro Tools 12 has made the software more accessible to more people. The number of my students who have access to Pro Tools at home has increased two- to three-fold since the Pro Tools 12 release. And I'm seeing a corresponding increase in student scores and classroom success as a result.

The cloud collaboration features in Pro Tools 12.5 take student learning and productivity to a whole new level. My students can now work on team projects remotely, access their projects at any time from anywhere, and submit their work to me without the hassle of transferring large media files. I am able to provide feedback to my students using the Artist Chat window directly within their Pro Tools projects, helping them identify and correct issues early on. There is a level of excitement for the product today that I haven't seen for years.

> —Frank D. Cook, president of NextPoint Training, Inc.,
> Pro Tools author, Avid master instructor, and adjunct professor
> at American River College in Sacramento, California

The digital resource pool is also benefiting from the open source movement. Applications like the Blender 3D computer graphics suite put sophisticated capabilities into the hands of any individual with a computer and broadband access and is very popular with game developers. Following in the footsteps of other open-source initiatives, such as Linux, this is prompting commercial software companies to compete by adding greater value to their products—a win-win for users.

The upshot of this trend toward lower prices is that individuals and small work groups are now able to produce extremely high-quality results, and platforms like YouTube, CD Baby, and Kindle Direct Publishing make it easier to bring that content directly to consumers, bypassing traditional media company relationships. It's also changing the economics of the mainstream media industry by lowering barriers to technology adoption. Media companies stand to gain business agility as a result—agility they need badly in order to adapt to the increasingly challenging digital media marketplace.

But for many, there's a significant downside. There are two important, and interrelated, trends. First, the barrier to entry has gotten far lower thanks to tools that are simpler, less expensive, and more available. This has led directly to the second trend: increased competition that has made it even harder for aspiring artists and smaller organizations to make money. In 2015, the six major studios generated 93 percent of the total box office revenue in North America; legions of independents had to split the rest.[4] The harsh reality is that even entrants at well-known events like Sundance are unlikely to experience meaningful commercial success.

A Storyteller's Perspective: Technology Is Not Just for Technicians

The "commoditization" of technology within TV news production has been long heralded, but it remains a work in progress. A string of developments over the past couple of decades has brought better access to such technology—for example, self-shooting with small cameras, desktop and laptop editing, and file-based systems that enable the free exchange of material and publishing. But we still have a ways to go.

Smartphones, the Internet, ever-rising metrics, and falling costs of accessible technology that have happened over the past twenty years have totally redefined what "commodity" means—and what users expect in terms of capability and ease of use. And it's certainly demystified technology—we have a large community of tech-savvy (and expectant) users now.

These means of production put publishing into the hands of those that create it (journalists), with ready access to tools that have the benefits of mass-produced consumer technology—familiar, cheap, capable, easy to use, ubiquitous, and reliable—and with a short and affordable renewal cycle. They demystify some technical processes and provide broader access to the necessary technology for production. And, most profoundly of all, they change "publishing" itself—not just inclusive of familiar linear broadcasting, with its specific teams and systems, but in the exploding and content-hungry world of online and social media.

So over the years, we've come a long way. The challenge for us now is to really harness that and bring it into the world of broadcast.

Let's not forget some of these innovations first appeared in newsrooms. Using BASYS systems in the 1980s, journalists relied on being able to instantly exchange electronic memos and send text messages to each other on their terminals and computers, which is a huge enabler that newsrooms have taken for granted. That was long before emailing and instant messaging became established (or the terms even familiar). I had to wait until the mid-'90s before I got corporate email.

Like commoditization, the demise of broadcast news has long been predicted but has never happened. In reality, modern TV newsrooms still thrive but have to serve the linear world of broadcast as well as online and social media. And that diverse world is the future we need to build for.

But there can be two very different worlds existing under the same newsroom roof. Online production is a largely commodity-product-driven affair, often with tools very different from the bespoke, big capitalized infrastructure, with specialized production teams that serve the linear broadcast world of studio production. And we still often culturally separate the two in newsrooms.

That is a challenge for the future for all technology managers now—aligning those worlds, and sharing acquisition and production processes (and culture), as much as possible. "Big tin" investments may always be necessary—up to a point—for something as customized as a live news studio. But it's that world that will need to be ever slicker, cheaper, agile, and less tailored to coexist in a world of commodity technology.

People are increasingly technically literate, and they expect technology to be slick and familiar. They expect to change it every couple of years for something much better. Now, there is a challenge for technology and finance directors investing in linear TV operations!

—Paul Stevenson, director of technology and technical
operations, ITV News

SIMPLER, FASTER, MORE EFFICIENT

Increased access to professional-level capabilities has simplified certain aspects of the content creation workflow in important ways. Video editing, for example, is far more efficient because it is nonlinear and increasingly conducted online via a service-based framework.

Audio is going in the same direction. The Avid Everywhere shared services platform, for example, makes Pro Tools capabilities available online, allowing musicians, producers, editors, and engineers to work entirely outside the traditional studio environment and workflow.

There's a problem, though, and it comes from legacy processes. Earlier we noted how, as the industry grew, steps in the chain from the content creator to the consumer were grouped to add scale, then technology was infused to automate each step. That worked very well before digitization and connectivity. But now that the chain can be entirely digital, the industry spends too much time and effort connecting elements in the workflow to accommodate today's business requirements. The fact is that digital files have a lot in common with one another, but without agreed-upon standards for things like file format and asset management, there's a lot of wasted effort and expense because companies keep on having to reinvent the wheel just to make all the pieces work together.

Any digital asset or process that is part of the production workflow can be made available via a cloud-based, shared-services platform that individuals from different organizations can plug into. Anything from music notation to mixing tools to video libraries can be deployed in this way.

Cloud computing, with its ready, low-cost, rapid scalability and low capital investment requirements, is sweeping the global economy and having a major impact on media. Cloud providers such as Amazon Web Services, Microsoft Azure, Alibaba, Tencent, and Google are already making major plays to be the cloud provider for all of media. Through the cloud, media companies can move rapidly from desktop creative tools to versions in the cloud, such as Adobe Premier, Avid Media Composer for editing, Pro Tools for music mixing, and solutions for newsroom technology, asset management, storage, and virtual and augmented reality—there's no technical reason why any system or digital business process cannot be deployed in the cloud.

The idea of services that can be shared shows great promise because it can help content creators and media companies alike overcome the issues that are driving imbalances in the industry. It holds the potential to enable a return to differentiation based on creativity and quality—great content— rather than better execution of a distribution and monetization model.

The shared services model is gaining traction and is, I believe, the key to the media industry's ability to move forward into a sustainable future. We'll take a closer look at the impact of this development in Part 4 of this book.

THE RESULT: AN EXPLOSION OF CONTENT

With content so much easier and less expensive to produce, the floodgates have opened. On the surface, it looks like content creation is thriving:

- 4,105 feature films and 8,061 shorts were submitted to the Sundance Film Festival in 2015, up from 1,059 and 1,479, respectively, in 1998 (CAGRs: 8 percent and 10 percent)[5, 6]

- 409 scripted television shows made it to air in 2015, up from 217 in 2010 (CAGR: 14 percent)[7]

- 43 million tracks were available in the iTunes catalog in 2015, up from 8 million in 2008 (CAGR: 27 percent)[8]

- ASCAP and BMI musician enrollments in 2014 were 525,000 and 650,000, respectively, up from 315,000 and 350,000, respectively, in 2007 (CAGRs: 8 percent and 9 percent)[9, 10]

- 396,000 games were available through the iTunes App Store in July 2015, up from 35,000 in July 2010 (CAGR: 62 percent)[11]

- 28,000 podcasts were hosted by Libsyn in 2015, up from 12,000 in 2012 (CAGR: 33 percent)[12]

If one considers how sluggish overall economic growth has been during these years (real GDP growth from 2005 to 2015 was 1.4 percent),[13] the growth in content availability and content creator interest is impressive indeed. To be sure, there are factors other than content creation at work—for example, growth in the iTunes catalog is due in part to the acquisition of rights to existing material. Nevertheless, it is clear that the pipeline is full to overflowing.

Is that a good thing? Yes and no.

It's positive in that media consumers have tremendous choice, but it's harder to decide what to consume. For the industry, there's a greater ability to tell stories, but there's more competition and costs involved.

The dark side is that it's increasingly difficult to make a living as a content creator and increasingly difficult to turn a profit as a media company. The economics don't work. The industry is out of balance, with more and more of the money being made by fewer and fewer people. That does not bode well for the future.

A Storyteller's Perspective: Valuing the Storyteller in the Digital Age

Music is, and always has been, made from the heart, and it stems from a passion that comes from the artist. When you're sad, happy, confused, or frustrated, you turn to music to bring you joy. That leads to this question: What is the market rate of joy?

When you think about economics, at its core, it is the relationship of resources between people and their contributions. If you contribute to something, like a mainstream song, you should be compensated. However, this form of economy has been greatly impacted by technology, and, in turn, it has hurt the artists, the ones making music for others to enjoy. The economics of music have become drastically disproportional.

People think music is cheap because it's easy to access, but it's not. If you think about everything needed to make quality music, you'll realize how expensive it is—on average, one song costs at least $100,000 to produce, advertise, promote, and market with the right image. Before technology brought the Internet to your fingertips, you had to wait in line at a store to buy music. Now, you can go out and spend $3,000 on a computer, and go home to buy a hit single for 99 cents or listen to it through a streaming service. So effective is this model that the economics that go into creating the content versus the market value of receiving content have already been toppled.

This is why the economics of the music industry have negatively impacted artists. Let's take Pharrell Williams's song "Happy," for example. It plays through a streaming service, which is free to many, 40 million times, and Pharrell generates a few thousand dollars in royalties. Now compare that to selling 800 CDs, which is clearly more valuable than having 40 million plays on a streaming service. You see, we are effectively fractionalizing the market value of content through the digital stratosphere. While technology makes it easier to create music, it also makes it easier to take music.

If an artist spends $100,000 to make a song but no one truly buys it, then the lights will go out in the studio space, and the equipment he uses to produce the music won't be updated. Music is one of the only luxuries that you can skip out on payment. If you know creating a song costs money, why would you take it for free? Some may think, "Why should I support those artists? They have money already." But it's not about the artists having money; it's about them providing the image and entertainment (the music) that costs money.

It's a win-win when people appreciate music enough to pay for it. It supports artists and gives them the means to afford the resources they need to produce it and bring you joy. Without that support, they cannot perform at their best and cannot offer you one of those true pleasures in life that you rely on daily.

—Jesse Wilson, music producer for Snoop Dogg, Justin Bieber, Ne-Yo, Celine Dion, *Birth of a Nation, Empire,* and many more

CHAPTER 12

At the Heart of the Dilemma: An Imbalance of Investment

I'm going to make him an offer he can't refuse.

—From *The Godfather*

The numbers show that investment in the tools and technologies that enable content creation is lagging behind the growth of the content itself. Yet both overall media industry budgets and content consumption are growing strongly. What's going on?

The answer is that media companies are facing a new and challenging competitive landscape, and in order to survive, they're doing all they can to chase profit. That means pouring money into monetizing content, often of existing properties. The ultimate losers are the content creators, because those investments in monetization aren't benefitting them in proportion to the rise in overall consumption.

This is what lies at the center of the current unsustainable situation. All players are getting squeezed. Media companies are driven to meet insatiable demand in ways they're not prepared for, and artists are getting shut out even as they produce more material. It's easier than ever to tell stories, but it's harder than ever to make doing so economically viable. That's the storyteller's dilemma (see image on following page).

NEW PRIORITIES: THE CONSEQUENCE OF THE DIGITAL AGE

The big issue is that distribution and optimizing the value of an asset has gotten a lot more complicated and expensive as digitization has accelerated.

Given that content is still king, prioritizing monetization seems a counter-intuitive strategy, but viewed from a different perspective it's understandable. The formula for creating content is well established. It's monetizing content profitably that has become so challenging, so that's where investment needs to go. Even the most successful media companies and professionals with proud histories are bowing to the pressure. No one is immune. How is it possible to

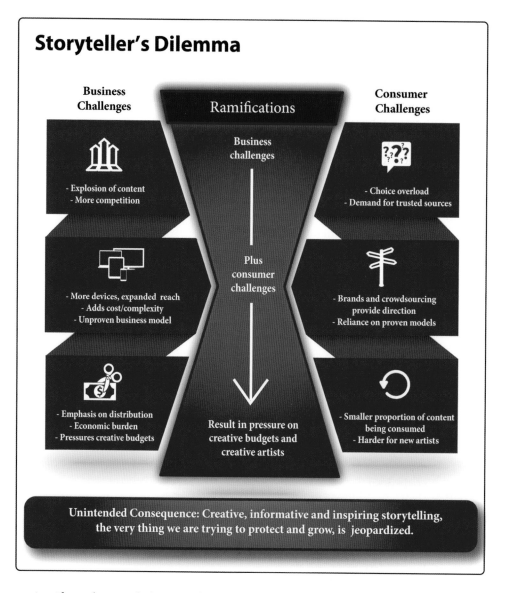

justify such an imbalance? I believe it's because media companies feel they must tackle the biggest challenges first.

Earlier we saw how workflows and processes evolved along with the growth of the industry, first being scaled up, then automated and connected. In media, that evolution involved massive investments that are now becoming a liability and forcing companies into uncomfortable investment choices.

In television, for example, the far-reaching broadcast networks that are core to the business are proving to be a costly infrastructure that must be maintained in the face of changing consumption habits and more agile competitors. Building on their heritage of great storytelling, broadcasters are adapting to new distribution and economic realities by reducing costs in traditional areas where revenues such as ad rates are under pressure, while investing heavily in digital distribution and monetization.

Think about your reality if you are in the media business today. From 2009 to 2015, the business environment supported growth in total technology spending of approximately 2 percent.[1] In exchange for this increase in spending, you'd have to increase content by up to 300 percent[2] in order to keep the lights on. In addition, to remain competitive in the face of rapidly advancing technology, you'd have to increase the number of channels, devices, and formats through which this content is available to the tune of almost 1,000 percent. And along the way, you have to maintain quality, maximize economic value, support your whole distribution network, and make it all run efficiently. That 2 percent increase in spending has to go a very long way indeed.

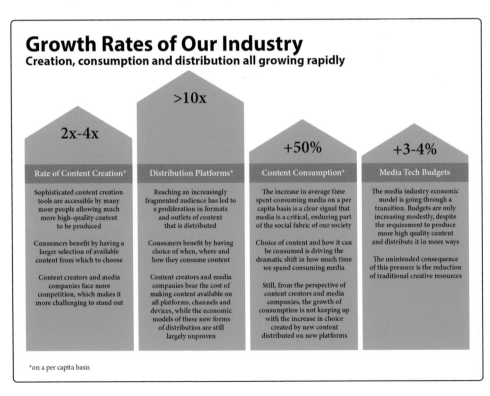

Growth Rates of Our Industry

Creation, consumption and distribution all growing rapidly

2x-4x	>10x	+50%	+3-4%
Rate of Content Creation*	Distribution Platforms*	Content Consumption*	Media Tech Budgets
Sophisticated content creation tools are accessible by many more people allowing much more high-quality content to be produced	Reaching an increasingly fragmented audience has led to a proliferation in formats and outlets of content that is distributed	The increase in average time spent consuming media on a per capita basis is a clear signal that media is a critical, enduring part of the social fabric of our society	The media industry economic model is going through a transition. Budgets are only increasing modestly, despite the requirement to produce more high quality content and distribute it in more ways
Consumers benefit by having a larger selection of available content from which to choose	Consumers benefit by having choice of when, where and how they consume content	Choice of content and how it can be consumed is driving the dramatic shift in how much time we spend consuming media	The unintended consequence of this pressure is the reduction of traditional creative resources
Content creators and media companies face more competition, which makes it more challenging to stand out	Content creators and media companies bear the cost of making content available on all platforms, channels and devices, while the economic models of these new forms of distribution are still largely unproven	Still, from the perspective of content creators and media companies, the growth of consumption is not keeping up with the increase in choice created by new content distributed on new platforms	

*on a per capita basis

WHERE'S THE COMPLEXITY COMING FROM?

A big part of the challenge is that media companies have more problems to solve today. In other words, what's dominating the conversation is the cost of doing business in a digital age, not the actual stories that the companies are in the business of selling.

We covered what's driving these costs in earlier chapters. Rising consumption is offset by increasing choice in distribution, device and platform, leading to less growth for any given channel. That in turn means that asset value must be optimized to sustain operations and support increasingly complex distribution.

It's no surprise then that when you look at where investment must go to make the business viable, you are seeing greater increases in spending on areas directly related to storage, archiving and retrieval, digital distribution, and monetization. There's double-digit spending growth in areas such as:

- Metadata tagging that allows you to track and reuse assets quickly

- Digital distribution models to get it to more people via more channels

- Distribution rights management to optimize the value of each asset component

- Media asset management, including storage, archiving, and retrieval technology to make sure you can access the content easily at any time, and tools to repurpose each asset quickly to optimize the revenue from various sources

- Distribution technology so that you can make it available immediately in many formats

- Open connectivity tools that lower the cost of integrating disparate systems

- Collaboration tools that allow you to work with the best talent anywhere around the world

As a proportion, lower spending is occurring on the actual creative process, though many of the creative tools are also enjoying modest growth. This is not surprising given how much content must be produced. However, in some hardware-based legacy infrastructure areas, such as the cabling used to transport high-definition video, investment is dropping rapidly as digital distribution models become more entrenched and enterprises adopt newer technologies to lower costs in an effort to fund the increased spending on distribution and monetization.

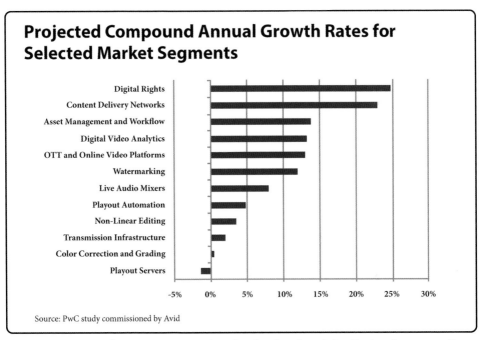

Projected Compound Annual Growth Rates for Selected Market Segments

Source: PwC study commissioned by Avid

Investment growth is strong in areas directly related to digital distribution, but not traditional models.

AN EVER-TIGHTER REVENUE PICTURE

Adding to the pain felt by media companies is the specter of decreasing revenue from their distribution channels. Digital transformation is causing traditional forms of distribution that earn higher revenues, such as CD retail sales, to be replaced by less mature models with much tighter margins, such as streaming.

Lower margins are a consequence of the effect technology has had on consumer expectations. Today, competition is driven by choice in all its

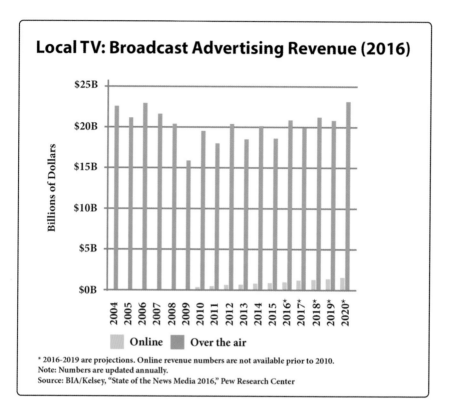

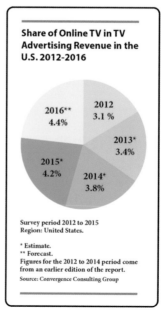

forms: choice of content, choice of channel, choice of delivery platform, and choice of pricing and consumption models. This is creating a dramatically different reality for traditional media industry players, and they must scramble to keep up. It can be a zero-sum game, where consumers win because they get more choice, but the industry loses because it has to provide those choices.

The only way to stay ahead in this environment is to drive up consumption, and the only way to do that is to fill every possible channel with more choices and try to rise above the noise. Forced to adapt quickly, the companies are expending great effort to make sure they meet the shifting needs of the market.

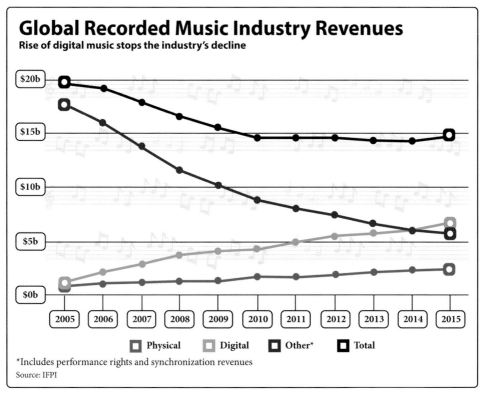

The rise of digitization has been a mixed blessing for the music industry. While it has offset the decline in revenue from CD sales, it has not delivered hoped for overall growth. Revenues have been flat for years.

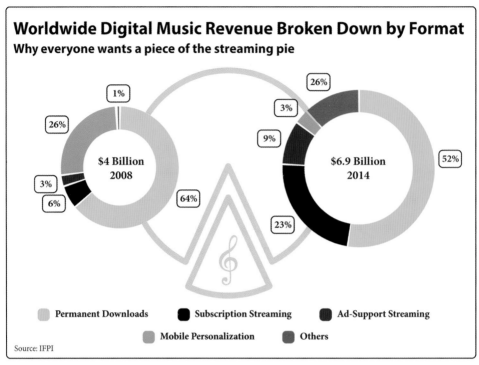

Worldwide Digital Music Revenue Broken Down by Format
Why everyone wants a piece of the streaming pie

$4 Billion 2008

$6.9 Billion 2014

Permanent Downloads　　Subscription Streaming　　Ad-Support Streaming

Mobile Personalization　　Others

Source: IFPI

Streaming is exploding in popularity, but that means increased complexity to support the shift to new channels. Companies must invest heavily to remain relevant.

CHOICE DRIVES COMPLEXITY, IN BUSINESS AND THE MARKETPLACE

Let's take a closer look at this phenomenon. In the past decade or so, the number of media outlets and technologies have increased dramatically due to broadband Internet access. That's prompted more and more competitors to jump into the market, experimenting with various distribution and monetization models as they try to one-up each other. The orderly picture of broadcast media distribution, whether over the air or via cable, is long gone.

In August 2016, Time Warner announced it was acquiring a 10 percent stake in Hulu at a valuation of $5.8 billion (three times Hulu's valuation in 2012). As part of the deal, Time Warner's channels, including TNT, TBS, CNN, Cartoon Network, and Turner Classic Movies, would be available on Hulu's new service set to launch in early 2017. That same month, Disney invested $1 billion to acquire a 33 percent interest in MLB Advanced

Media's spin-off media company, BAMTech. As part of the deal, BAMTech will collaborate with ESPN to launch a "multi-sport" subscription streaming service.

Today, we have subscription-based streaming video on demand from Netflix, Amazon Prime, and Hulu, plus ad-supported video on demand from players like YouTube, Facebook, Vimeo, and Vine. Pay-TV brands like HBO, Dish, Sling TV, and CBS All-Access are also providing programming outside of conventional cable services. And there are new crossover services, like streaming access to expanded content for cable subscribers to create second-screen or multi-screen experiences. Creating and maintaining these services, and filling them with content, is both complex and costly, which prompts media companies to allocate an increasing proportion of budgets to these activities.

It has been challenging for traditional media companies to migrate their businesses to accommodate this digital transition. Consider the case of ESPN, one of the most successful brands of all time and a category creator in sports broadcasting. In August 2015, Disney disclosed that it had lost pay-TV subscribers and was reducing profit projections for its media networks, notably including ESPN (according to Nielsen data, ESPN had lost 7 million subscribers in the prior two years). The resulting investor sell-off over two days reduced the public market value of Disney by $22 billion. Despite this, ESPN chief John Skipper noted that ESPN had 100 million unique visitors a month on its digital platforms and was approaching $500 million in digital revenue. Unfortunately, relative to the linear television declines and resulting investor reaction, this digital stream of revenue was a virtual drop in the ocean.

In music, the digital shift has been to streaming, and the top two services in terms of paid subscribers are Spotify with 30 million and Apple Music with 15 million.[3,4,5] These services are driving an increasing share of industry revenue. In 2010, streaming accounted for 7 percent of overall revenue. In 2015, it made up 34.3 percent, surpassing digital downloads of 34.0 percent for the first time ever.[6]

Unsurprisingly, media companies are doing everything they can to capture that growth, and as we've seen, that's what's driving the current imbalance in investment. It's also what's making life so difficult for content creators, who must reach many more consumers if they are to make money. It's no wonder that artist compensation is down even as streaming revenue skyrockets.

What does it take to earn $1,000 as a content creator?

| 362 CDs* | 4,392 audio downloads** | 100,000 to 1+ million streams*** |

*CDs: Assumes a retail price of $12.00 and signed artist share of 23%.
**Audio Downloads: Assumes a single track download price of $0.99 and signed artist share of 23%.
***Streams: Based on disclosed average per stream payouts of various streaming providers.
 Assumes signed artist share of 20%.

Source: Based on selected assumptions aggregated by David McCandless, http://www.informationisbeautiful.net

The proliferation of channels isn't the only thing adding to complexity. While on the surface, it may seem that technology has simplified and streamlined production and distribution because it's now possible to connect and collaborate online, digitization has in fact added new requirements.

With no single standard for workflows, individual processes, and technologies, production is far from simple. Collaborators—whether individuals or media companies—may have to waste considerable effort aligning with one another simply because they don't operate the same way using the same tools.

The same misalignment happens up and down the value chain. For any given distribution platform, digital assets need to be identified, securely and reliably transmitted and stored, converted into multiple video and/or audio formats, and embedded with additional metadata for digital rights and asset management. And that's just the tip of the iceberg. The processes needed to monetize an asset through one channel might not match another channel's demands, and internal use, such as news footage archiving and playout—the transmission of content from the broadcaster to its network—might add yet another layer of technical and procedural requirements.

When these activities are viewed on a global scale, they become major challenges. Even when as much of this additional activity as possible is automated, the overall process remains much more complicated than it used to be. And every additional step adds to cost.

HOW THE NEW ENVIRONMENT IMPACTS INVESTMENT

Broadcast industry spending trends illustrate the dilemma that media companies face. According to IABM and Devoncroft's *2016 Global Market Valuation Report*, from 2009 to 2015, acquisition and production spending rose by a CAGR of only 3 percent, spending in the post-production segment was flat, and playout and delivery spending fell by a CAGR of –3 percent. Bear in mind that for the same period, content growth was in double digits.[7]

But over the same period, according to the report, spending on nontraditional services like online video platforms, "over the top" (i.e., content delivery over the Internet), content delivery networks, video on demand, and infrastructure to support it all grew in each case at a CAGR in excess of 10 percent. That's money that did not go to content creation.[8]

This imbalance is growing. The IABM/Devoncroft report noted that in 2009, there was a 1:7 ratio of spending on these nontraditional services relative to the combined spending on acquisition and production, post-production, and playout and delivery segments. By 2015, that ratio was 1:3.[9]

These changes in the flow of funding are both a symptom and a cause. With more and lower-cost ways to create and distribute media now available, new entrants have entered the fray, and traditional players are adapting by building on their heritage and positing themselves for the digital age. Because the economics of a pure-play digital platform generate lower returns while also being more complicated, it's a difficult transition, but consumption patterns and economic realities are forcing traditional players to move in this direction, requiring a change in strategy.

As the digital media landscape becomes more diverse and competition for consumer attention intensifies, it takes massive investment to keep up and generate positive returns. Everyone in the media ecosystem is adjusting—some faster than others—as they try to position themselves for the next phase of the media industry.

We've seen the transition to digital formats in music radically change that segment, which is now only recovering through live events and improving economics. As we've outlined, however, there is a disequilibrium, and the biggest losers are the artists themselves. It becomes more and more difficult to adapt while still keeping the existing business running. The pressure to pull more funding away from content creation is relentless and rising.

CHAPTER 13

Defining the Problem: What Makes Things So Difficult?

Houston, we have a problem.

—From *Apollo 13*

The rapid pace of technological change and channel proliferation has put the industry in a difficult position. Companies across the spectrum are faced with the need to adapt very quickly to new requirements and shifts in distribution and monetization models. At the same time, they're getting squeezed from the other end by flat revenue as the number of choices dilutes the value of established channels and properties.

The basic problem is the complexity of adapting to the new environment. Assets must be produced in multiple formats, archived, tagged, managed, distributed, and monetized over a wide variety of platforms as quickly and efficiently as possible. And as roles in the media workflow become less vertical—in other words, as individual stakeholders get directly involved in more of the overall process—this complexity impacts more and more people.

For example, a solo artist trying to make a few dollars from creating and selling recordings must now worry about the technical details of distribution, file formats and optimization, metadata, digital rights management, payment . . . and a host of issues brought on by digitization. Media companies have the same challenges on a vastly larger scale, and others besides, including archiving, routing content for playout, and tailoring assets for specialized uses.

A Storyteller's Perspective: Distributing to Audiences Everywhere Across New and Old Platforms

Big Brother *began in the reality TV boom. It started in the Netherlands in 1999 and is now on in more than twenty countries, including the United States, where the show is in its eighteenth season at the time of this writing. It was a huge hit in Europe, but localizing the show for each region wasn't without its challenges, which gets to the heart of the storytelling happening beneath what seems on the surface a reality game show. In its European form, it's more about the discussions between housemates; Americans like to see action and competition.*

Throughout the eighteen seasons of Big Brother, *we have provided a variety of ways that the audience can experience the show. There are three weekly traditional, one-hour shows that are broadcast on the CBS television network. Each evening,* Big Brother After Dark *is available on our cable channel POP (this was originally shown on Showtime), and viewers can also subscribe to a streaming service that allows them to watch live uncensored feeds from the* Big Brother *house twenty-four hours a day. Viewers of the streaming service can watch any of four video streams from the* Big Brother *house. There are more than a dozen "houseguests" who are living in the house with no contact with the outside world; sixty cameras follow their every move, and all the houseguests wear microphones at all times. The four video streams represent the four story lines going on in the house. For example: Stream one may be showing three houseguests in the kitchen; stream two may show several houseguests by the pool; stream three may show houseguests talking in the bedroom; and stream four may show houseguests playing a game in the living room.*

In addition, houseguests who get voted out of the Big Brother *house are interviewed, and these interviews are made available on CBS.com. CBS also briefly contributed to a mobile service and provided* Big Brother *directly to mobile devices, but this service was discontinued. There are also* Big Brother *social media websites, where people predict what will happen next or chat about something that is going on in the house. This dialogue around* Big Brother *has created a community of people who are connected around the show. For people following the show on social media, it fuels their desire to watch and see if the things they guessed would actually happen.*

It's certainly a unique show, as it airs for three months each summer and consistently gets high ratings. The show's distribution model perfectly illustrates how we don't really consider ourselves a pure broadcasting company anymore, but rather more of a content provider that will offer content any way consumers want to experience it.

—Barry Zegel, senior vice president & general manager,
CBS Television City

PROCESS EVOLUTION IN THE MEDIA INDUSTRY

The complex and multifaceted process of creating, distributing, and monetizing content is constantly evolving—not just for storytellers, but also for anyone who serves any function at any stage, all the way from creation to consumption.

Whether you're a content creator, media producer, distributor, or consumer, or you fill some other contributing role, you execute one or more steps in the media value chain. As with any kind of value chain, it begins with an idea, and the final deliverable is a product. That product could be a book, recording, broadcast, performance, film, or work of art—any kind of content that an audience can consume.

Traditional media workflows evolved before digitization changed the game. What began as a relatively simple exchange between creators and consumers became a series of highly structured production and distribution processes that encompassed the entire industry. Over the course of the twentieth century, dozens of steps that included conceiving, producing, formatting, marketing, distributing, and monetizing media came to resemble assembly-line production. To ensure that creative professionals were rewarded for their efforts, the business side of the media industry became almost as important as creativity itself.

In the previous section of this book, we saw how advances in technology drove the evolution of processes in business and industry. The same forces are at work in the media industry; the business of telling stories has adopted many of the same operational models and processes as every other enterprise that produces and distributes a product. In other words, the media industry has followed the same trends as other businesses in terms of production processes, automating, and focusing each step in the value chain to increase efficiency.

As the various industries in the media ecosystem grew, they established what were, at the time, sustainable creation and monetization models that could be scaled. Roles in the media workflow became well defined (and siloed) and the economic power of the industry became well established.

Regardless of the form of media, whether a motion picture, a news broadcast, a scripted television show, or a song or musical score, repeatable processes for creation and monetization were created, each supported by a viable economic model.

Steps in the chain were clearly defined and dovetailed with one another. Media organizations aligned to optimize the overall workflow in order to allow the individuals and the enterprises involved to continue doing what they loved.

Over time, these business models continued to be refined, and along the way, profits grew. The many media industry segments enjoyed strong success by following similar models, finding an effective process to provide the stories that met the market's increasing desire to be informed, inspired, and educated.

Just as with other industries, as technology advances occurred all along the media value chain from pre- to post-production and distribution, enterprises began adopting or creating technologies to automate each step in the process. Breakthrough technologies at every level began to emerge, and the entire workflow accelerated and became more efficient. But at the core, the processes were not changing; rather, they were being refined to a high degree.

Not very long ago, the workflow of creating content, formatting it for numerous devices, marketing it, distributing it for public consumption, and monetizing it required specialized tools and talents every step of the way. Many companies and individuals still do things that way. Even though the entire workflow can be digitized and in theory streamlined, we're left with the remnants of a siloed, disconnected world, cobbled together from a complex web of servers, cables, middleware, and proprietary software.

Probably the biggest waste is that when the processes were grouped and then automated, most were based on proprietary programs developed by vendors with a narrow focus on their specialty. Media participants then built their own proprietary applications and infrastructure to support both internal and external parts of the process.

The upshot was massive duplication of effort across the industry. Many vendors and clients built equivalent processes that were unique, even though they were largely producing the same output. Also, a great deal of time is spent simply connecting the pieces of these proprietary components together and getting them to work smoothly.

This dated approach and infrastructure is one of the biggest contributors to the current economic imbalance, because media companies have to invest in distribution and monetization and are saddled with older workflows that are inflexible and expensive to maintain and connect.

In an environment of changing economics, where speed and agility is critical and greater efficiency is a must, this is an untenable situation. This is especially true when you consider that now the entire workflow can be digitized and more of the processes are similar and can be shared not just within different groups in a given organization but across people, groups, and organizations, interchangeably, around the world.

DIGITIZATION MUDDIES THE WATERS

Rapid technological development on the production side put stress on these established processes and models. Digitization blurred the lines. Unlike industries that produce physical products, such as cars or consumer goods, the entire media workflow can be digital from start to finish. Because of this, advances in connectivity, processing speeds, and other technologies are having a more profound impact on the media industry than is the case elsewhere. There is the potential for new technologies to be much more disruptive to the traditional workflow and the underlying business model. Those that struggle to adapt are left at a significant disadvantage.

To an informed observer, the implications are clear. The well-honed business models, processes, and workflows that once supported content creation and distribution need to catch up, and keep up, with advancements on the production side.

But the issue isn't just the processes themselves; it's the natural inertia inherent in the value chain developed to create and distribute content. The various steps in the value chain had specific needs as the story moved along the workflow to the consumer. As these processes were grouped and automated, they could be optimized and enjoy economies of scale because they were able to leverage the predictable nature of how money was made. This fostered a system where the primary difference was the quality of the content itself—helped, of course, by the marketing and distribution engine that existed at the time.

Digitization turned this on its head because there are new requirements, new connections, more complexity, and less predictability. In the digital world, the media value chain has only grown more complex. Each discrete step requires its own supporting technology, and the workflows are not always well integrated. In many cases, that technology has become so specialized that it has driven up production and distribution costs.

If we could start fresh in an environment where the entire connection can be digital, we would probably create an entirely new process with fewer steps, fewer handoffs, and a more streamlined, integrated approach with fewer disconnects that separate the storyteller and the consumer. The emerging digital channels provide a clear example where, from creation to consumption, things can be more streamlined and simple.

THE DIRECT DIGITAL CONNECTION

Throughout the twentieth century, most artists and content creators relied on others to connect them with their audiences, and many of the most successful ones still do. Publishers connected writers with their readers, and record companies connected musicians with their fans. Filmmakers needed an army of personnel to bring their visions to life and monetize their dreams. Movie studios and theaters made the profitable connection between filmmakers and the cinema-going public. Although those same connections still exist today, that paradigm is changing rapidly due to digital acceleration. The connection between the creator and the consumer has become more direct.

A Storyteller's Perspective: Embracing a New Viewpoint

To this day, film is still romantic from a consumer and creative perspective, and that should never change if we do our job right. However, while we continue to harness this romanticism with film, we are simultaneously romanticizing the technology and production processes of yesterday instead of embracing the technology of today. We need to stop looking back and instead look to the future and the path technology is paving ahead.

This is all about embracing the new and gaining insight into how we should work as an industry, not always how we do work. We cannot let our old production vehicles tie us down, and need to accept the fact that they had their moment in time.

—Darren Long, director, Sky Production Services

The digital connection between the production of creative content and its consumption has changed everything about the business of media—including the need for traditional processes. Gone are the days when you needed one team of people to record your song or produce your video, more people to design the packaging and manufacture the CD or DVD, and even more people working as store clerks who actually put your song or video into consumers' hands.

Back then, everyone had their own discrete piece of the workflow, but the tools that technology makes available to everyone now have forever changed that old-fashioned, one-step-at-a-time approach. Economic pressures are forcing the industry to automate the connection between the creative and the distribution processes, and technology is making that possible. As noted earlier, however, that automation is not enough to offset the rising complexity that's skewing investment in favor of monetization.

The actual rate of change depends largely on the media organization's culture. I've observed that those with a corporate culture that favors stability and proven methods tend to resist change, only moving when forced to. This can put them at a disadvantage; those with a more change-oriented culture are quicker to move, and the economics tend to reinforce and validate those decisions. These are the companies that, in my view, are more likely to thrive in the future.

DIGITAL MISALIGNMENT AND ITS IMPACT

One of the primary reasons why the media value chain is suffering so much from complexity is a lack of agreement on basic standards. Steve Jobs famously refused to support Adobe Flash on Apple devices, for example, leaving gaps in the user experience.

The upshot of this lack of standardization is that budgets are disproportionately slanted toward the mechanics of format conversion, digital rights management, asset protection, marketing, and distribution. Because too many people in the media industry still cling to old, sometimes proprietary ways of doing business, costs in these areas needlessly increase for almost everyone.

Those who create content don't usually spend their own time and money reformatting it for incompatible standards. They're focusing on creating new and better stories, as they should be. For that reason, the marketplace has filled a niche translating digital files between incompatible platforms. Converting digitized media from one format to another and making it compatible with many different output devices is big business. An increasing proportion of media budgets is dedicated to making sure that media files run smoothly on any device a consumer may prefer, whether it's a high-definition television, a laptop, a tablet, or a smartphone from any of the dozens of manufacturers that make such devices. Without these kinds of translation technologies, music you listen to or movies you watch on your Android smartphone might not be compatible with your Apple iPad. In some cases, translation and optimization is built into software, or may be provided by a hosting service such as YouTube. That makes life easier for some, but it leads to still more complexity and cost.

KEEPING A HANDLE ON ASSETS: THE NEED FOR METADATA

Along with reconciling incompatible standards, media providers must deal with issues such as tagging, rights management, and security. The explosion of available media has made it absolutely necessary to embed metadata (information about what a file contains) within media files so that these assets can be managed throughout their life cycle.

From the consumer's perspective, keywords are necessary to locate the right media from an overwhelming assortment of choices. Without some means of filtering metadata, searching for content would be a much more frustrating and time-consuming experience than it is today.

Metadata tags are used for a variety of other reasons on the production side and are essential for digital manipulation of content. Most people involved in content creation are familiar with the editorial tools for enhancing and modifying a scene, but in a digital world, tags can be used for all parts for the value chain, including advertising and marketing. For example, metadata can be used to tag every scene where a given character is wearing a blue jacket so that effects artists can change the color to red. Or it can be used to flag any scene where there is a particular brand of soft drink and replace the can with a beer bottle.

During production, metadata allows editors to tie pieces of content together to tell a better story more efficiently. This is critical for news organizations, which must accurately tag a constant flow of content for later retrieval, editing, and distribution—often in near-real time, because the window of opportunity between an event taking place and broadcast is very short.

From the artist's and copyright owner's perspective, the most important role of metadata is making sure that wherever a media file goes, it includes information about who created it and who has the ownership rights. This information is critical for rights management—who should get paid for what is consumed and how usage is managed (a single-use license vs. unlimited use in a specific capacity, for example). There's also the need to lock down content to prevent piracy. Without digital rights management and security software in place, there would be no way to ensure that content creators and distributors would ever be paid for their work. DRM controls who and what can access creative content, preventing it from being copied and freely distributed, consumed, or altered without authorization.

COMBATING THE PIRACY PLAGUE

Before the age of digital media, rights management wasn't as critical an issue as it has become. When the industry was more profitable, a certain amount of leakage was tolerable, and technology was on the side of the rights holders. While anyone with an audiocassette recorder could create an inferior copy of a commercial recording, and anyone with a VCR could make a low-resolution duplicate of a movie or television broadcast, it was usually much easier to simply purchase an authorized copy. This ensured that content creators and distributors would be paid for their efforts; the loss due to piracy was relatively small. But now that it's so easy to make a perfect digital copy of just about anything, DRM is absolutely essential. With the economics of the industry not nearly as good as they once were, this issue is far more important.

With digitization came peer-to-peer file sharing, and all of a sudden, piracy threatened the very existence of the media industry. A sense of entitlement to "free" content, driven by the Internet, led to plunging sales revenue. Albums that would have sold over a million units in the past only sold a couple of hundred thousand, and an album that would once have generated enough revenue to sustain a band until they could produce their next album no longer yielded enough to cover its production costs. That forced artists to raise concert ticket prices in order to make up the difference, and they've skyrocketed since.

Security technology, not DRM, is going to be the biggest contributor to the solution. The fact is that people are going to try to get, and use, content for free whenever they can, and DRM is not going to alter that behavior. People are not likely to do the right thing by choice, and it's not possible to enforce a right if the technical means to manage it are not in place. Technologies such as encryption, digital watermarking, and random separation are examples of such tools.

With security technology catching up with pirated assets, the industry is recovering somewhat from the peak of the piracy problem, but it persists because so far, work-arounds have been easy to find.

There have been some interesting solutions to this dilemma. A subtle and clever one has cropped up on YouTube; if you create a video and use a commercial song for its sound track, the service detects it and will allow the upload, but only if you agree to display a small banner ad along with the video. The proceeds of the ad are shared with the copyright holder. This is an example of a win-win solution. The uploader gets to use that favorite song, YouTube makes money, and so does the artist. Attempted piracy has been turned into a profit opportunity, with little impact on user experience.

Counterbalancing this is YouTube's stance that it has no direct control over what is posted. Even with revenue-sharing schemes like the one above, it's easy to find pirated content from users who have found ways to bypass YouTube's controls. Clearly, work remains to be done on the piracy front; these nascent attempts to recapture value pale in comparison to the economic damage done to artists.

OPTIMIZING VALUE TO GET MORE OUT OF EVERY ASSET

In today's world, content creators can't just produce and distribute great media. We also need to optimize its value over longer periods of time than in previous generations. The ability to reformat and repackage content for different audiences and devices makes it desirable to extend its life. Optimizing value means getting more revenue out of every asset, creating an opportunity that's obviously attractive to anyone in the media industry.

In the old days (with certain exceptions), once you'd created media in a specific format, pushed it out to the network, and put it on the shelf, you were done with it. With the proliferation of media formats, however, all that has changed forever. When we create content now, we need to anticipate all the various ways it might be used in the future. It might someday be used in hundreds of ways that are impossible to anticipate. We need to put ourselves in a position that if we need to call on an asset down the road, it will be available more quickly. We also need to make it easier to optimize for every conceivable format.

As you're creating a media asset, metadata tagging becomes a lot more important if you want the ability to quickly repurpose it. Tagging could make it easier for someone to shorten or augment an asset to fit different formats, for example, or make it easier to insert ads. Tagging is key if you want someone to someday reuse an asset and reformat it without jumping through too many hoops.

With content being repurposed, repackaged, redistributed, and resold in endless combinations, the legal complications of compensating rights holders can quickly become unmanageable. Digitization has added a new twist, because through metadata it is possible to embed information in digitized assets that enables greater accountability and oversight.

For example, the music on a given television show might have been licensed for five years. What happens if the show gets rebroadcast twenty years later? Is anyone even aware of the original license? Is the rights holder going to know that the music is being used, or will an opportunity for license revenue go untapped? With digital tagging of the music, it's much easier to tackle that issue. The music could be overdubbed to avoid paying an additional license fee, or the license could be renewed.

There's also the question of actively protecting the asset once it's released. Copyright owners must constantly scan for pirated material and block or remove it from circulation, taking legal action when necessary. Online checks and balances for tracking, accountability, and payment must also be put in place to ensure proper compensation.

The biggest challenge is determining who is actually responsible for all of this. Individual content creators are in a poor position to fully understand

and enable digital rights management, yet they need to be aware of its full implications. Media companies are in a better place, but they may not have the interests of their content creators as their first priority.

"No Coke. Pepsi."

Here's just one small example of how digitization simultaneously makes the life of a media professional both simpler and more complex. Let's say you made a film with a Coke can in one of the scenes, but the film is being distributed through a channel that has a deal with Pepsi and doesn't allow any media with Coke in it. "Tagging" the can would make it easier to digitally airbrush it out or even replace it with another product. There would be no need to reshoot the scene at great expense—but the software, processes, and skills must be in place to make it happen. This is not the kind of thing that can be accomplished on the fly in an economically feasible way.

FROM A BROKEN MODEL TO ONE THAT SERVES ALL OF US

In its current state, the media value chain has become so disjointed that it's economically unsustainable. The economic models that connect storytellers with their audiences are unnecessarily inefficient. Fortunately, it's within our grasp to make immediate changes that will vastly improve the situation, leading to better economics for not just everyone in the media industry but for audiences as well.

Having someone to facilitate the exchange between creators and distributors still has advantages, but it has to be done in a more efficient way that automates lower-level functions to maintain and enhance whatever motivates storytellers to do what they do best: informing, inspiring, educating, and entertaining their audiences.

Because we have not taken advantage of what's possible, we're living with a needlessly disconnected, segmented, complicated technology infrastructure that is outdated and is unnecessarily adding to cost.

Fortunately, at the same moment that media has become such a prominent force in our lives, innovative software platforms allow us to break down the walls that separate the various stages of production, both in manufacturing and in content creation and distribution. As we gradually dismantle the walls, we'll come to realize that we don't need walls at all. Although the end result is greater efficiency and lower cost, some players are slow to adapt or resistant to change, and that's where the problem lies.

PART 4

Where Can We Go from Here? A Vision for the Future

CHAPTER 14

The Case for a Common Platform

Roads? Where we're going, we don't need roads.
—From *Back to the Future*

Throughout this book, we've explored the issues facing the media industry and their consequences. The problems are difficult to solve, and many are systemic. Yet they are not impossible to overcome.

Let's start with a clean sheet and ask what's needed. The whole point of storytelling is to connect with the audience. In a digitized world, that joy can occur more directly, more efficiently, and more powerfully. The steps in the workflows created at the dawn of the media industry, later automated through technology and connected to increase efficiency, would be entirely reengineered if we were to completely redesign them today.

Think about the advantage that a purely digital media company has. The files that it creates and distributes don't have to move through inefficient digital silos built around manual processes. That company has the luxury of moving more directly through steps in the workflow from content creator to the consumer, focusing only on applications and activities that make the story or connection better, not on legacy activities rooted in the romanticized era that the workflow was originally created for. This allows the company to focus on the business challenges of creating the best content and connecting to audiences in the most efficient way possible.

But many traditional companies are still dealing with the baggage of the past. It's more than romance that holds them back. It's an antiquated system that costs the industry money and, more importantly, siphons dollars from the creative process. With competition more intense than ever, a company burdened by an inflexible infrastructure, filled with proprietary connections and suboptimal steps, can ill afford to pile more on to these heritage processes in order to accommodate new channels.

In a fully digitized world, we can reimagine how we create and connect. If all that was common about the digital file's journey were shared by applications, by people, by processes, and by other businesses in the value chain, we could focus on spending time and money on what makes us unique, not what is the same. This is the core argument for common standards that all can benefit from.

The future is about much more than how you create. In the future, how you create will impact how you connect and monetize media assets. Since this is the key issue, it's vitally important to find a way to make that entire creation-connection-monetization cycle simpler, more efficient, and more equitable.

I believe the way forward lies in creating a shared-services platform that all participants in the media value chain can tap into. A set of technologies, processes, formats, and standards that is universally recognized and highly automated becomes a useful resource, not a source of added cost and complexity.

This can't happen overnight. An interim step is needed in which practical, real-world solutions allow participants at every point in the value chain to continue to use the tools they prefer, yet be able to connect everything so that resources are freed. As we've seen, one of the biggest issues facing the media industry is disconnected, redundant workflows based on proprietary technologies. It's too complicated to get things done because processes, services, and assets differ at various points in the value chain. There's tremendous incompatibility that must be overcome, duplication of effort that drives up cost, and needless complexity.

Driven by economic reality, there's been a lot of discussion in the industry lately about connecting these tools and technologies. The groups that define and codify industry standards—of which Avid is an active member—are working to standardize the myriad proprietary tools that are the basis of the siloed processes that continue to dominate much of the industry.

While I agree that connecting these embedded proprietary technologies can create cost savings, I believe that over the long term it is preferable to adopt open standards-based tools across the value chain. That holds the potential for far greater overall cost savings and innovation.

At the end of the day, storytellers still need the most effective tools at every step of the workflow: the most powerful digital editors, the best storage, the most effective media management, the most flexible news-gathering tools, and all the rest. But to deliver on the true potential of digitization and collaboration, all of these tools need to be fully integrated so they can work better and more efficiently. The key is seamless integration that comes from the platform itself, much as the operating system in your smartphone provides a common infrastructure that apps use to deliver the experiences that users desire. The value-add doesn't come from the platform; it comes from the creativity of the app designers. The focus is on what differentiates, not the low-level, automated services built into the shared ecosystem.

A Storyteller's Perspective: The Right Tool for the Job

From a broadcaster's point of view, we must accept that we need to move at great speed and commoditize things we currently do. We have a certain quality threshold to maintain, but we must also be willing to take calculated chances. If we were an Internet start-up, how would we move forward? By embracing the new and even designing it.

Technology in the broadcast world doesn't have to be gold-plated. Use what's right for the job and what you know will entertain your customers. Begin to step away from the old way of building a broadcast and look at where we get the most value. That may be through nontraditional broadcast technologies, which can enable us to put value where it is needed, not where we're used to having it.

Suppliers and manufacturers must also follow our cue, be agile, and always look forward. We are moving away from being hardware driven. Now what we continue to need is software that is easily accessible on a platform with applications and services available from multiple suppliers. This also gives us a means to share key information that companies do not like to part with: data. It's the secret sauce of every company and what we guard strongly. However, it has been shown that opening up and collaborating with other manufacturers is working! Tracking and analyzing data together enables us to see how customers are using our content to ensure that all we do has value.

Are we taking advantage of what vehicles will give us the most value and how that is being measured? When we deliver content to our customers, we must keep in mind that we determine monetization value not just by the number of viewers but also through social media and other popular media channels.

Beyond collaborating among ourselves, we must work with emerging content creators, even if they don't fit the standard mold we've become accustomed to. New and traditional content providers can work side by side and ultimately entertain viewers, which is the end goal. At the same time, we need to lose our fear of Google, Facebook, YouTube, and other channels. What they don't have yet is access to the people you do, and what they have is power and reach across global audiences. Join forces with these companies, understand their needs, and work together in partnership.

We also need to think about how to incorporate social media into our storytelling process at the start of every project, not as an afterthought. Social media is free marketing. People are self-perpetuating it and creating marketing that you never imagined. It's the best way of marketing content; don't overlook this opportunity.

As we look ahead, we must remember that what we do for the industry is for our customers and viewers, and not to glorify who we are or what we do. We need to stop forgetting what we're here for—to deliver entertaining content to our customers, not to stand on a podium and romanticize about the past. We are genuinely here to produce content that our customers love and to tell a memorable story.

Whatever we do, it's always about great storytelling. We need to follow the rules of storytelling—draw in customers and make them want more. That's when success is realized.

—Darren Long, director, Sky Production Services

REMEMBER THE BAD OLD DAYS?

The situation is not unlike the way things used to be in personal computing. Years ago, people bought personal computer hardware and software at retail. You'd buy a box with a CD-ROM in it, bring it home, load it, have issues, spend time on the phone, learn that it may not work with your peripherals, and you'd have to go find new drivers for those peripherals. Maybe you couldn't get it to work properly at all, and the file formats might not be compatible with anything else. Often, an update in the software or peripherals would break something and make you gun-shy. Once you finally got everything working, you didn't want to touch it again for fear it wouldn't work.

In the 1990s, we were in the midst of the browser wars. A website might or might not work with a given browser, which made web development a real nightmare—complicated and difficult.

It's very different today. Now we have shared standards, and it doesn't really matter much which computer platform, application, or browser you use.

Applications share common resources and focus on an activity that improves your life. Software-as-a-service applications, like Google Docs, take standardization a step further, creating a simple, unified experience. A single sign-on accesses a broad suite of applications that are well integrated and compatible with the *de facto* Microsoft Office standard. What goes on behind the scenes in terms of file management and integration is based on shared services. It's easy and ubiquitous and radically expands choice and flexibility. It also provides the flexibility to decide how you want to engage with the platform, what apps are most useful to you, and which one you like better.

WHAT A SHARED SERVICES PLATFORM LOOKS LIKE

Because of digitization, the different parts of the media industry aren't really different anymore. In the grand scheme of things, media is media; there are many common elements. Looked at this way, at a certain level there really is no difference between producing an album and making a movie or a TV show. Both involve digitized files. Both involve processes for tagging, archiving, digital editing, transporting data, and monetizing assets.

Content is one thing. The underlying technologies are something else, and digitization has brought with it the opportunity for convergence. So there's no technical reason why there can't be common processes, standards, and workflows. By introducing uniformity and commonality across all parts of the media industry, everything can become simpler. Therefore the ideas of a shared services platform and open standards-based tools make sense. Connecting the creative processes to consumption by the user more directly, more profoundly, and more powerfully has the potential to make the distribution of revenue and value far more equitable.

It is important to not only share what is common but to integrate the tools themselves. You still need the technologies to create, tag, store, manage, distribute, and monetize, even if they're based wholly on open standards. While we always want to work with the best tool for a particular function, such as editing or mixing, the larger business issue is not using a "better" editor or mixing technology; it's integrating the tools you choose to adopt with lower-cost common services and resources and making it all work together efficiently that's critical. With open standards, the value added by specialized tools that are unique to a particular step in the process can be retained while at the same time more easily integrated into the workflow. We need not give up anything to gain the productivity and cost benefits that open standards can provide.

The biggest reason why the standards and technologies that a shared platform is built on should be open is so that no one organization can unilaterally control any part of the value chain. Software companies would thus be free to create compatible tools based on clearly defined standards, knowing that interoperability is guaranteed. All standards should be accessible so that any participant can benefit from them and compete on a level playing field. This way, whether it's multiple artists collaborating on a song, a media company working with one of those artists, or a media company licensing that song to another media company, the underlying infrastructure connecting them together is shared. That leads to much lower overall costs.

Such a platform should encompass the core common technologies that are shared by all parts of the media industry—metadata standards, file formats, conversion, indexing, resolution, adaptability, optimization processes, and the like. These are the very things that add cost and complexity to current workflows, but which do not allow companies or artists to differentiate themselves. They are not sources of competitive advantage.

The platform should also be constantly reviewed and updated to accommodate technological advances. Rather than being a static construct, it should be a living thing that evolves in parallel to the digital world, supporting those who do business there.

THE IDEA OF AN OPEN PLATFORM IS NOT NEW

This concept of common platforms and open standards is well established, and it works. The concept is familiar to any computer user. USB peripherals are plug and play, because hardware manufacturers adhere to the published standard. Websites work seamlessly across devices and computer platforms thanks to HTML, and IP addresses make global connectivity possible. Agreement, formalized or not, is how technology is able to function.

Shared services (like domain-name lookup), data feeds (such as weather and stock prices accessible via open programming interfaces), and Google search that can be added to any website simply by copying and pasting a few lines of HTML code are commonplace. There are other, less-familiar open standards and shared services that enable enterprises to add value at low or no cost.

The common thread is that all of these resources are non-proprietary and accessible to anyone. The same functions could be performed in a proprietary way, but there's really no point. They do not differentiate or add unique value.

What Does "Open" Mean?

Open standard—An industry-wide, agreed-upon, and published definition for anything from file formats to communications protocols to processes that is accessible to all. Any product or service that adheres to a given standard will be compatible with any other that also complies. An open standard can be defined by a public or private organization, but many are managed by industry groups.

Open source—A licensing scheme that prevents users of intellectual property from profiting by reselling it. It is a legal framework, not a technical one.

Shared service—A utility or function that is accessible to all so that people need not create it themselves. Shared services may or may not be free to use, but they do guarantee consistency and compatibility.

Open standards and shared services are not the same thing as open source. They can be controlled by a company, and many are. Apple, for example, is notorious for keeping a tight rein on what developers are allowed to sell in the App Store. Every application must meet strict standards. But the resources and shared services that are the building blocks of those apps are readily available, so developers need not spend time and effort creating everything that goes into their work. They're able to devote their energies to creativity and quality instead.

If the media industry were to fully embrace open standards and shared services, all participants would be able to connect common elements and have the freedom to use the creative tools that they want. By sharing common services, and by being able to connect any tool from creative to distribution to these common services, we get the best of all worlds. It becomes possible to reduce costs, increase value, and optimize resources so that the true joy of storytelling can shine through.

Differentiating on What Matters: The Story of Linux

One of the best examples of how the "open" concept benefits the industry as well as end users comes from business computing: the Linux operating system. As the world of commerce became increasingly dependent on computers, a robust operating system called UNIX came to dominate business computing. There were multiple "flavors" of UNIX, all proprietary and licensed by major corporations such as IBM (AIX), Sun (Solaris), and HP (HP-UX). These operating systems carried hefty end-user license fees.

What this did was generate a lot of cash for the big computer firms, at the expense of the businesses who were forced to license the operating system. What it did not do was create an incentive for innovation or differentiation based on added value. The operating system license arrangement was a cash cow that sucked up resources better used elsewhere.

In the early 1990s, a revolution took place, building on the idea of open-source software that had begun to gain traction. A Finnish software engineer named Linus Torvalds released the kernel of Linux—an open-source version of UNIX—under public license. Developers were free to download and modify it and use it as they saw fit. The only thing they could not do was resell it.

What this did was extraordinary. Linux became a mainstay operating system for business computing at the highest levels. Unable to make any money from the operating system itself, companies were forced to differentiate themselves in other ways—by adding value in the form of services, for example, or developing innovative application software.

The beauty of open standards is that they eliminate so much effort. It's not necessary to reinvent the wheel; the standards are there for anyone to use, so the whole technology-dependent economy becomes vastly more efficient. Anyone who develops a product based on open standards knows that it will be compatible with all other products that follow the standard out of the box. Less time is spent integrating and more is spent on the power of the tools themselves.

Think of what this means for tools to create, distribute, and monetize media content. The same idea can extend to automated processes and workflows. Any low-level function or standard can be commoditized and shared so that all may benefit from it equally.

Common tools also lower the cost of innovation, provide more flexibility to adapt, and offer simpler ways to integrate with the media value chain. In effect, they help to create an ecosystem in which everyone can participate at a dramatically lower cost.

ACCELERATING A NATURAL PROCESS

While the imposition of an open shared-services platform might seem authoritarian and anti-competitive, in fact it is not. All it does is accelerate what happens naturally.

Traditionally, the marketplace decides what the standard is to be. Eventually, businesses converge and settle on one way of doing things. Getting there, though, can be a painful and expensive process, and often the "better" technology does not win. The battle between VHS and Betamax is one example. Betamax had better resolution, slightly better sound, and a more stable image, but VHS won because longer recording times were possible and the hardware was cheaper.

Competing standards can make life difficult for both consumers and businesses. At the height of the desktop computing battle between Apple's Macintosh and PCs, there were incompatible hardware interfaces for peripherals, such as mice, keyboards, and printers. That meant manufacturers had to produce two versions of every product if they wanted to cover the market. Many didn't, choosing to support only PCs because that platform had more market share. Users of the less-widespread Macintosh platform were left with fewer choices. The arrival of a shared, open standard—USB—eliminated those issues, and both businesses and consumers benefitted. This kind of competitive shakeout is inevitable over time.

Today's software tools are more open and compatible than they once were, allowing for lower cost and easier integration. Nevertheless, competing standards still impact us, and they are at the root of much of the cost and complexity faced by consumers and the media industry. If all participants in media—including device makers, service providers, and content creators—were to agree on a simpler set of standards, the situation could improve greatly.

What if the entire back end of media were shared? Competitiveness could actually improve, because subscribing to the common platform would simplify the overall workflow for everyone. What if costs dropped so low that it became economically feasible to experiment with different approaches, rather than commit to a costly proprietary set of technologies? All that would be left to differentiate is the best stories and easiest and lowest-cost way to consume. Companies would compete on quality because their resources would not be tied up in low-level activities, and it would be easier to collaborate with others since differences would be eliminated. All we'd be doing by adopting shared services is eliminating wasted effort for the whole industry. Wouldn't that be better for everyone?

CHAPTER 15

Why Changing the Way Things Are Matters to All of Us

Let's get together and feel all right.

—Bob Marley

We've seen how digitization and connectivity have created new challenges for the media industry and caused it to become unbalanced. But it does work, after a fashion. Consumers enjoy low prices, there's greater choice, and more content is getting produced. Anyone can find almost anything they want and consume it in the way they choose. So what's the rationale for shaking things up?

The short answer is that we're all wasting time, energy, and money on things that should not, and need not, matter—things like simply connecting the pieces of disjointed proprietary systems, reformatting files for a constantly evolving set of formats, or correctly naming and tagging files so that they can be located and leveraged.

Today, we're forced to connect files and processes remotely and securely through a seemingly endless set of new applications and disconnected pieces. These digital files move through myriad handoffs, databases, and tools that at their core do many of the same things, thus draining dollars and resources and in the process siphoning money away from critical activities that add value.

By working in this way as we try to cope with changes in the industry, we are seeing an unintended consequence. Namely, a shift in focus away from the very thing that brings joy to people: the story itself. At the end of the day, it's the content that matters. Even if you can reach every person in the world, what does it matter if stories themselves—stories that advance our social fabric—are found wanting?

If we look at the whole process of storytelling in the digital age, from the initial idea to the final enjoyment of that story, we see a vast and complicated web. There are tools, processes, agreements, and standards involved, with many roles, connections, and dependencies. There's a whole ecosystem of services that support the industry.

But pause for a moment and think of it this way: There are elements of this picture that separate and differentiate us, and other elements that don't. Talent, quality, and the consumer experience separate participants in media. These are the things that should be used to differentiate us. The lower-level functions of file formats, data transmission, archiving, metadata tagging, DRM . . . these are the same for everyone, everywhere. And those are the very things that are consuming more than their fair share of time, money, and effort from the beginning of the value chain to the end.

If we eliminate the things that don't separate us—those common elements—we can focus on the things that *do* differentiate us. There is no good reason why we can't simplify and automate those lower-level functions and make them, in effect, invisible.

STEP BACK AND ASK WHAT MATTERS

What is actually gained by having multiple formats, processes, and standards? What does the complexity buy us? In the end, storytellers want to use the best tools to express themselves, and their audiences want to experience stories when, where, and how they wish, without having to worry about the details. What happens in between should not matter. So why have we collectively created an environment in which those irrelevant aspects dominate our thinking?

It's All About the Outcome

Several years ago, a colleague of mine had the pleasure of meeting Dr. Amar Bose, whose company has long been known for taking alternative approaches to audio. During an address, Dr. Bose spoke of the company's design philosophy.

Bose was a student at MIT and a lover of classical music. He was disappointed in the quality of sound reproduction at the time, and when he had the opportunity, he purchased the best hi-fi system he could, expecting it to be far better than what he'd previously experienced. It wasn't. He realized then that the focus on the technical details, such as frequency response, amplifier power, distortion, speaker sizes—all the specs that dominated the marketing and selection of equipment—were a distraction. What really mattered was the performance at one end and the reproduced sound at the other, not what was taking place in the middle. The technical details were not relevant to the experience, and sometimes what looked better on paper didn't sound as good. That epiphany became a guiding principle for the company.

These are important questions. The technology infrastructure should not limit what is possible; the media workflow should only be limited by the imagination of the storyteller and the joy it brings to the audience. Everything else should be as streamlined and efficient as possible. In the end, the community dictates the value a good story brings, to inspire, educate, and inform. The tools to tell these stories should be as simple as the apps on your phone—all seamlessly connected, all using the same shared resources, all transparent.

WHY STORYTELLERS SHOULD CARE

In an age of digitized storytelling, technology is an almost inescapable part of content creation. That's an important aspect of the expanding role of the storyteller we covered in Part 1. In order to share the joy of storytelling, the artist has to pay attention to how that story gets out into the world.

Technology is also an important part of the creative process. Software tools and computer interfaces are used to capture and edit performances, both audio and video, so that what leaves the storyteller's hands is of remarkably high quality. Artists want the best tools, and rightly so.

But that doesn't mean they should be burdened with needless complexity. The tools they use are a differentiator that helps them express themselves better, so that should be where their energies and time are focused. Storytellers should not have to concern themselves with anything other than practicing their craft. Low-level processes and the gritty details of file optimization, protection, and monetization aren't their core competency. Those aspects can, and should be, automated and take place behind the scenes—and if those tools are connected to standardized shared services, content creators can be free to choose those that meet their needs best.

If the industry as a whole adopts more efficient shared services and standards, there would be knock-on effects that benefit the storyteller. Content creators should recognize that how they create has an impact on how they monetize. If they create using tools that share a common ecosystem, they can automate the rest of the value chain. More dollars are then freed up for the creative process, where real value exists for them and the audience. Money that media companies now devote to operations, distribution, and monetization could then be invested in the artist without sacrificing profit. Better compensation means that more artists would see storytelling as a viable career choice and would have more incentive to stay in the game.

The community of talented individuals who share their joy would grow and be able to sustain itself. There would be more collaborators, more influences, more opportunity to create and deliver sights, sounds, and messages that surprise, delight, and enlighten.

So storytellers should care because a simpler, more efficient process that they need not get elbow-deep in—enabled through technology—lets them devote more attention to what they do best. They should care because it makes what they do easier. They should care because it frees up financial resources, so they can be rewarded for their talent and hard work—without damaging profits or driving costs up.

WHY MEDIA COMPANIES SHOULD CARE

Thus far we've thoroughly discussed the issues and challenges that digitization, connectivity, and changing consumer behavior create for the media industry. Companies are stuck in a morass of complexity and high costs, with outdated, disconnected processes chasing rapid technological change and disruptive business models. They're forced to devote too much capital to simply connecting all the pieces and on new distribution and monetization efforts.

For media companies, the case for a simpler way is straightforward. Anything that promises better efficiency, improved business agility, and lower costs should be welcome. Clearing away dysfunctional methods is an opportunity for a better bottom line, and the chance to reallocate capital to add value rather than squeeze every last bit of return from their properties. With increased freedom and discretionary income, they can invest where it counts—in better content.

So media companies should care because less complexity in the form of standards, formats, platforms, distribution, and monetization lets them devote their resources to differentiating themselves instead of treading water. They should care because it will improve their ability to respond to new developments in technology and consumer demand. They should care because simplification adds to profit, not cost. They should care because it lets them build a more sustainable business, built on a stronger pipeline of high-quality content made available to more people that will yield rewards for many years to come.

WHY INDUSTRY PROFESSIONALS SHOULD CARE

When a media professional like a sound engineer or film editor starts spending as much time on technical issues as on shaping the story, something is fundamentally flawed. In many ways, that describes the current state of affairs. The reality of working in the industry is not what many imagine it to be. The devil is in the details, and it's all details. There isn't as much opportunity to add value as one might think, simply because the daily routine gets in the way.

How you create impacts how you monetize. Professionals will always want the best tools, but they no longer have the luxury of worrying only about product quality—sound, image, or any other form of digital experience. If it costs more money down the line than it earns because it wasn't optimized in the first place, sooner or later you're going to go out of business. Since the whole chain from content creator to consumer is digital, even if you only want to focus on your part of the chain, how you create impacts the degree to which you can optimize the asset. That's where tools that connect to a common, global ecosystem can be so much more efficient and effective. If while you are in the process of creation, you can automate metadata tagging, standardize reformatting, index assets—any of the process steps that are essential in a digital world—your product can be repurposed and optimized all along the value chain without more work. This impacts budget allocation up and down the value chain—and ultimately how much can be spent on creation.

Automating routine processes, rationalizing technical requirements, and simplifying workflows allow media professionals of all kinds to work smarter and pay more attention to quality. That ability to make a lasting mark and generate something that stands apart is why many of these individuals chose media as a career in the first place.

So media professionals should care because a simpler, streamlined, more productive environment makes their lives much easier and makes their business more sustainable. They should care because it lets them make positive contributions rather than get caught up in process details that do little more than move product through the system. They should care because it opens the door to a far more satisfying career and makes the stories they help tell more valuable over time.

WHY CONSUMERS SHOULD CARE

At a fundamental level, consumers are concerned with only two things: getting what they want and paying the lowest price for it. But in reality, there's more to it than that.

While consumers may not be thinking in terms of platforms, formats, or business processes directly, these things are nevertheless of great importance because of their impact on the things that consumers do care about. Consumers, it is often said, vote with their wallets. Whoever has the most attractive balance of quality, selection, and price wins business.

Consumers routinely run into issues because of format wars and content availability. One delivery platform might offer something they want but not another. Their chosen device might not support a particular content provider. They may have to pay for content they don't want to get content they do want. From the consumer's point of view, all of these issues are off-putting. Where's the benefit in forcing these unpopular choices on them?

When things are made simpler and less costly for the media companies and storytellers that consumers give their money to, options, quality, and selection can go up and prices can come down, without negative impact on the businesses or the storytellers. The consumer wins, and so does the industry because customers are happier.

So consumers should care because a system that runs more efficiently and is simpler makes their experience better. They should care because they can freely choose whatever device, service, and content pleases them. They should care because they see their favorite artists being treated fairly. They should care because they'll see a wider variety of new, high-quality content to entertain, enlighten, and educate them.

WHY SOCIETY SHOULD CARE

Helping the media industry find a way to navigate this complicated landscape and emerge fulfilling the role that we all care about can impact society on a large and far-reaching scale. By helping companies compete on added value rather than monetization, a better-functioning industry promotes economic activity and growth. That adds jobs. And as the industry grows, the efficiency of a simpler system pumps money into the creative end, encouraging more people to get involved.

When the balance of investment shifts back toward content development and away from the "business of business," the quality of what we see and hear can go up. We get greater diversity, more varied opinions, more depth and meaning in the stories we hear. Our lives—all of our lives, whether we're in the industry or not—can improve as a result.

So legislators and the public at large should care because a media landscape where creativity and storytelling are valued more than they are today benefits us all. We should all care because it can lead to more, and more rewarding, jobs. We should all care because it's a better way to spend our money. We should all care because what we create today will influence what our children experience in years to come.

Part of this generation's role is to ensure that the enduring social fabric of storytelling will remain a thriving part of our culture and future. We know it connects us, advances us, and allows us to deal with issues important to all. Storytelling is able to play this vital part in society because there is a certain romance in connecting to the deep well of shared experiences that has been part of the human experience since before the written word.

THE TIME TO ACT IS NOW

As a professional who interacts with and serves every part of the vast global media industry on a daily basis, it is clear to me that the way it functions needs to change. Sharing the joy of stories is part of our social fabric and always has been. It's up to each generation to carry that human tradition forward, and this is our way to contribute and create a renaissance of great storytelling.

The future can be bright, the industry can be profitable, and the storytellers who are so much a part of our lives can be properly rewarded for the wonderful contributions they make. I'm very optimistic that all of these outcomes can be achieved, if we take a clear-eyed and rational look at how things are done. We need to focus on what adds value. We must think about what makes us unique, rather than consume all our time, resources, and attention dealing with short-term issues.

From where I sit, adopting standards and sharing services is the most viable way to accomplish this, the one that will benefit everyone—storyteller, audience, and everyone in between. I believe that going in this direction is imperative, because in the current climate of digital acceleration, we no longer have the luxury of waiting for the marketplace to sort things out. The world is moving too fast, and the penalty of moving in the wrong direction is too great.

It is far better to get ahead of the issue, determine what separates us and what we have in common, and create a climate in which we all share and benefit from the stories that tie us together. That's what will allow us to enable the joy of storytelling to continue for years to come, and it's in our power to make it happen.

Acknowledgments

Many people were involved in bringing this book to life, and I am deeply indebted to all of them for their advice, assistance, and patience. First, I'd like to thank Andrew Douglas for his assistance in the creation of *The Storyteller's Dilemma*.

I particularly appreciate the support and insights I received from my many friends and colleagues in the media industry, and the staff of Avid Technology, who made it possible to manage the demands of writing alongside the demands of running a company.

I'd like to extend my thanks to Stephen Stage and his team at Avid Technology for their countless hours in the coordination and completion of all of the different work streams. The team consisted of Sheryl Backstrom, Timory Burleson, Billy Gil, Sara Griggs, Mary Nielsen, Frank Quadro, Robert Roose, Maria Russo, and Kathryn Smith.

Some of the most successful creative artists and leaders of some of the largest and most influential media companies were kind enough to share their personal reflections on a variety of topics discussed in the book that provided unique behind-the-scenes insights on the transition the industry is navigating. For their stories and reflections, which appear throughout the book, I would like to thank Mohamed Abuagla, executive director of technology & operations, Al Jazeera Media Network; Sandra Adair, editor of *Boyhood* and *School of Rock*; Turki Al-dakhil, general manager, Alarabiya & Alhadath News Channels; Maryam Almheiri, CEO, twofour54; John Aranowicz; Guillaume Aubuchon, CIO DigitalFilm Tree; Alan Bell, A.C.E.; Andreas Bereczky, vice chair, ZDF German Television; Paula Boggs, founder of Boggs Media, board of directors for Avid Technology; Maryann Brandon, editor of *Star Wars Episode VII: The Force Awakens*; Butterscotch, music artist, finalist on *America's Got Talent*; Lindsay Chalmers, general manager of Enterprise Operations, Television New Zealand; Steve Cohen, A.C.E., editor of *Bosch, The Bridge, 15 minutes*; Frank D. Cook, president, NextPoint Training Inc.; Elizabeth Daley, dean of the USC School of Cinematic Arts; Maureen Drowney, managing director, The Recording Academy Producers & Engineers Wing; Charlie Feldman, vice president writer-publisher and industry relations, BMI; Richard Friedel, executive vice president and general manager, Fox Networks Engineering & Operations; Frank Governale, vice president of operations, CBS News; Eric Kuehnl, assistant director, music technology program at Foothill College; leadership at Fortress Plus Risk Management; Darren Long, director, Sky Production Services; Randy Magalski, editor of *Chainsaw*; David Mash, senior vice president for Innovation, Strategy, and Technology, Berklee College of Music; Fred Mattocks, general manager, English Services Media Operations, CBC; Mischke, songwriter/producer; Barak Moffitt, head of strategic operations, Universal Music Group; Mike Nuget, PostWorks New York; Delbert R. Parks III, senior vice president and chief technology officer, Sinclair Broadcast Group; Matt Schneider, PostWorks New York; Paul Sidoti, professional musician; Paul Stechly, president, Applied Electronics; Paul Stevenson, director of technology and technical operations, ITV News; Jason Stewart, editor of *The Amazing Race, The Voice, Extreme Makeover: Home Edition, World's Greatest Dad*, and *Sleeping Dogs Lie*; Herb Trawick, executive producer and co-host, *Pensado's Place*; Jesse Wilson, music producer for Snoop Dogg, Justin Bieber, Ne-Yo, Celine Dion, *Birth of a Nation, Empire*, and many more; and Barry Zegel, senior vice president and general manager, CBS Television City.

There also was some extensive research conducted by some key employees at Avid Technology. For their time and contributions, I would like to thank Regis Andre, Ofir Benovici, Tim Carroll, Tim Claman, Guillaume Godet, Rob Gonsalves, Michael Hale, Amir Hochfeld, Joel Lamdani, Randy Martens, Shailendra Mathur, Rich Nevens, Rob Scovill, and Craig Wilson.

There are many other people to whom I need to extend thanks for ideas, feedback, research, fact-checking, copyediting, proofreading, design, production, publicity, and promotion. You know who you are, and I deeply appreciate the contribution that each of you has made.

Notes

Foreword
[1] Natalie Donovan, "If CDs cost £8 where does the money go?" *BBC Magazine* website, August 26, 2013, http://www.bbc.com/news/magazine-23840744.
[2] Katie Marsal, "iTunes store a greater cash crop than Apple implies?" AppleInsider blog entry, April 23, 2007, http://appleinsider.com/articles/07/04/23/itunes_store_a_greater_cash_crop_than_apple_implies.html.
[3] Avid research.
[4] RIAA sales database, https://www.riaa.com/u-s-sales-database.

Chapter 3
[1] Facebook corporate website, http://newsroom.fb.com/company-info.
[2] U.S. Census Bureau, http://www.census.gov/population/international/data/countryrank/rank.php.
[3] Twitter corporate website, https://about.twitter.com/company/press/milestones.
[4] Instagram corporate website, https://www.instagram.com/press/?hl=en.
[5] *Broadcast Industry Global Market Valuation Report*, Devoncroft Partners, 2016, http://blog.devoncroft.com/broadcast-industry-market-sizing.
[6] LinkedIn corporate website, https://business.linkedin.com/talent-solutions/blog/2014/01/top-10-job-titles-that-didnt-exist-5-years-ago-infographic#!
[7] Nielsen Online press release, October 27, 2008. http://www.nielsen-online.com/pr/pr_081027.pdf.
[8] Douglas Macmillan, "Mobile Search Tops at Google," *Wall Street Journal Digits* blog, October 8, 2015, http://blogs.wsj.com/digits/2015/10/08/google-says-mobile-searches-surpass-those-on-pcs.
[9] "What is big data?" IBM website, https://www-01.ibm.com/software/data/bigdata/what-is-big-data.html.
[10] "America's Young Adults at 29: Labor Market Activity, Education and Partner Status: Results from a Longitudinal Survey," U.S. Bureau of Labor Statistics press release, April 8, 2016, http://www.bls.gov/news.release/nlsyth.nr0.htm.
[11] "Did You Know?" U.S. Department of Labor, 2013, http://www.bls.gov/spotlight/2013/tenure/home.htm.

Chapter 4
[1] The Numbers online database, http://www.the-numbers.com/movie/Cleopatra#tab=summary.
[2] Turner Classic Movies, http://www.tcm.com/this-month/article/102757%7C102758/Cleopatra.html.

[3] Joseph Schwartz, "Pokémon Go: The Data Behind America's Latest Obsession," *Digital Vision Data Billboard* blog, July 10, 2106, https://www.similarweb.com/blog/pokemon-go.

[4] "Pokémon Go teens stuck in cave 100ft underground," BBC News website, July 15, 2016, http://www.bbc.com/news/uk-england-wiltshire-36805615.

[5] "Two fall from bluff while playing Pokémon Go," Fox 5 San Diego website, July 14, 2016, http://fox5sandiego.com/2016/07/14/two-fall-from-bluff-while-playing-pokemon-go.

Chapter 5

[1] *U.S. Time Spent With Media,* eMarketer, 2014, https://sbmarketingstrategy.files.wordpress.com/2015/01/emarketer_us_time_spent_with_media-emarketers_updated_estimates_for_2014.pdf.

[2] Avid research, based on aggregated publicly available data from Apple, YouTube, *Variety*, and the Sundance Film Festival.

[3] Twitter 2015 United States Securities and Exchange Commission Form 10-K, https://www.sec.gov/Archives/edgar/data/1418091/000156459016013646/twtr-10k_20151231.htm.

Chapter 8

[1] RIAA sales database, https://www.riaa.com/u-s-sales-database.

[2] Ben Sisario, "CD-Loving Japan Resists Move to Online Music," *The New York Times* website, September 16, 2014, http://www.nytimes.com/2014/09/17/business/media/cd-loving-japan-resists-move-to-digital-music-.html.

[3] RIAA sales database, https://www.riaa.com/u-s-sales-database.

[4] Ibid.

[5] Twitter feed of Daniel Ek, CEO of Spotify, https://twitter.com/eldsjal/status/711927333071036416.

[6] Janko Roettgers, "Apple Music Now Has 15 Million Subscribers, Gets New App Design," *Variety*, June 13, 2016, http://variety.com/2016/digital/news/apple-music-revamp-1201794467.

[7] Matthew Rocco, "TV Deals Boost NFL Revenue to New Record," Fox Business website, July 21, 2105, http://www.foxbusiness.com/features/2015/07/21/tv-deals-boost-nfl-revenue-to-new-record.html.

[8] Ibid.

Chapter 9

[1] *The Total Audience Report Q4 2015*, Nielsen, 2016, http://www.nielsen.com/content/dam/corporate/us/en/reports-downloads/2016-reports/q4-2015-total-audience-report.pdf.

Chapter 10

[1] David Stout, "66 Journalists Killed in 2014: Report," *Time* website, December 16, 2014, http://time.com/3635440/journalism-reporters-without-border-murder-kidnapping.

[2] Avid research.

[3] Ibid.

[4] Matthew Ball, "The Digital Future of TV Networks & The Original Series Crunch," *Redef* blog, February 5, 2015, https://redef.com/original/the-digital-future-of-tv-networks-the-original-series-crunch.

[5] Cynthia Littleton, "Peak TV: Surge From Streaming Services, Cable Pushes 2015 Scripted Series Tally to 409," *Variety* website, http://variety.com/2015/tv/news/peak-tv-409-original-series-streaming-cable-1201663212.

[6] *2013: The Year in Rewind*, Nex Big Sound, 2013, https://www.nextbigsound.com/industry-report/2013.

[7] Glenn Peoples, "Recording Industry 2015: More Music Consumption and Less Money, That's Digital Deflation," *Billboard* website, January 7, 2016, http://www.billboard.com/articles/business/6835350/recorded-industry-2015-consumption-grew-revenues-digital-deflation.

Chapter 11

[1] Film/Video Editor Salary (United States), PayScale Human Capital website, 2016, http://www.payscale.com/research/US/Job=Film_%2F_Video_Editor/Salary.

[2] Avid research.

[3] Adobe blog, January 21, 2106, https://blogs.adobe.com/creativecloud/from-sundance-to-hollywood-more-filmmakers-than-ever-editing-with-premiere-pro-cc/?segment=dva.

[4] "Market share of leading film studios in North America in 2015," Statista website, http://www.statista.com/statistics/187171/market-share-of-film-studios-in-north-america-2010.

[5] Sabs Adij, "Sundance 2014: The festival by the numbers," New Slate Films website, January 12, 2014, http://newslatefilms.com/featured/independant-films-show-more-growth-in-2014-sundances-infographics-reveals-the-breakdown.

[6] "30 Years of Sundance Film Festival," Sundance Institute website, 2014, http://www.sundance.org/festivalhistory.

[7] Cynthia Littleton, "Peak TV: Surge From Streaming Services, Cable Pushes 2015 Scripted Series Tally to 409," *Variety* website, http://variety.com/2015/tv/news/peak-tv-409-original-series-streaming-cable-1201663212.

[8] Avid research based on Apple data.

[9] *2014 Annual Report*, ASCAP, 2014, http://www.ascap.com/~/media/files/pdf/about/annual-reports/ascap_annual_report_2014.pdf.

[10] *2014–2015 Annual Review*, BMI, 2015, http://www.bmi.com/pdfs/
publications/2015/BMI_Annual_Review_2015.pdf.

[11] "Number of available apps in the iTunes App Store from 2008 to 2016
(cumulative)," Statista website, July 2016, http://www.statista.com/
statistics/268251/number-of-apps-in-the-itunes-app-store-since-2008.

[12] Amy Mitchell and Jesse Holcomb, "State of the News Media 2016." Pew Research
Center, June 15, 2016, http://www.journalism.org/2016/06/15/state-of-the-news-
media-2016.

[13] Avid research, based on U.S. Bureau of Economic Analysis data.

Chapter 12

[1] *Broadcast Industry Global Market Valuation Report*, Devoncroft Partners, 2016,
http://blog.devoncroft.com/broadcast-industry-market-sizing.

[2] Avid research, based on aggregated publicly available data from Apple, YouTube,
Variety, and the Sundance Film Festival.

[3] Twitter feed of Daniel Ek, CEO of Spotify, https://twitter.com/eldsjal/
status/711927333071036416.

[4] Janko Roettgers, "Apple Music Now Has 15 Million Subscribers, Gets New App
Design," *Variety*, June 13, 2016, http://variety.com/2016/digital/news/apple-music-
revamp-1201794467.

[5] Ben Taylor, "By the Numbers: The Streaming Music War (and Who's Winning),"
Time website, August 14, 2014, http://time.com/3109273/streaming-music-
services-compared.

[6] Joshua Friedlander, *News and Notes on 2015 RIAA Shipment and Revenue
Statistics*, RIAA, 2015, https://www.riaa.com/wp-content/uploads/2016/03/
RIAA-2015-Year-End-shipments-memo.pdf.

[7] *Broadcast Industry Global Market Valuation Report*, Devoncroft Partners, 2016,
http://blog.devoncroft.com/broadcast-industry-market-sizing.

[8] Ibid.

[9] Ibid.

Index

technology
    access to tools, 22, 72, 115, 117, 150,
        163
    and creativity, 23, 41, 45, 65
    disruption, 25, 72
    and efficiency, 27, 67, 69
    definition and roots, 45
    impact on society, 51, 58, 62, 69, 76–77
Trawick, Herb, 62–63

video games, 11, 50, 65
Vietnam War, 5
virtual reality, 40, 48, 51, 54, 65

Wilson, Jesse, 45–46, 121–122
workflow, 28–29, 47, 57, 67, 71, 124, 132,
    137, 149, 161

Zegel, Barry, 135–136